Patches
A Wyoming Cow Pony
by
Clarence Hawkes

Illustrated by
Griswold Tyng

MILTON BRADLEY COMPANY
SPRINGFIELD - MASS.
1928

Bradley Quality Books

STRAIGHT INTO THE AIR HE BUCKED

CONTENTS

THE ROMANCE OF THE CATTLE LAND. INTRODUCTORY

LIST OF ILLUSTRATIONS

THE ROMANCE OF THE CATTLE LAND

I F you will examine a map of the United States printed
fifty years ago you will find a large tract of land between the Missouri River and California designated
as the Great American Desert. If you examine a recent
map of the same country you will be surprised to note
that this desert has entirely disappeared and that in its
place are half a dozen prosperous and populous states.

The truth is that the desert never really existed except in the imagination of the geographer, with the
exception of a small portion of Utah where there is
still some desert land.

After the Lewis and Clarke expedition up the
Missouri, and after the discovery of gold in California in
1849, a goodly number of adventurous spirits flocked
across the western plains in search of gold and adventure. These adventurers who were always fickle and
restless were shortly followed by a more serious-minded
company who were homemakers and settlers. The
thing that most vividly impressed these settlers on coming into this new El Dorado was the great herds of
bison grazing upon the western prairies.

These bison kept sleek and fat not only in the summer, but in the winter as well, and they subsisted merely
upon the bounty of nature.

11

Thus the question at once arose, if the bison could subsist in this way merely upon the bounty of nature, why could not cattle be raised in the same manner and thus get rid of the first cost of raising them.

So the western emigrant soon had small herds of cattle grazing upon the prairies just as the bison had done before them. These were the nuclei for the mighty herds of cattle in our western grazing land which finally made this nation the greatest beef-raising country in the world.

The root stock however, of this cattle raising industry had already been planted on this continent nearly two hundred years when the original "Texas Longhorn" was imported from Spain into Mexico. These long-horned, tall, gaunt cattle finally drifted across the Rio Grande into Texas, and thence up the Panhandle into New Mexico and what is now Oklahoma and still further north, so when the western settlers first came to the western prairies there were wild cattle grazing on the plains in the same herds with the bison.

From time to time the early cattle men introduced new stock of Durham, Hereford, and other large breeds and crossed them with the Texas Longhorn. The real Texas steer is a tall, rangy animal weighing when fat a thousand pounds.

Since the herds of cattle ran unrestrained upon the prairies the question of identification very early arose, so it was not long before branded cattle and cattle with either one or both ears slit appeared upon the prairies. At first these branding marks were rather simple, but it soon became apparent that they had to be more complicated as the cattle rustler who was the professional cattle thief could easily change simple markings. Thus the letter C could be changed into a G or a cipher, I could be easily changed to L, M to N and so on. This necessity for an elaborate mark soon led to a branding iron which was six or seven inches square and cattle were marked either on the shoulder or hind quarters, or both. Also in many cases the ears were slit as well. But even so the professional cattle thief or rustler grew bold and rich as well; this, notwithstanding the fact that the branding irons had been registered at the local county seats as soon as the particular district had a seat of government.

Since there were few sheriffs in the primitive west in those early days, and fewer courts and justice was very tardy, what was called necktie parties were very soon in vogue. This seemed the only way in which to deal with the professional rustler. These parties always took the form of a surprise party. In fact, the surprise of the recipient of such honors was usually beyond words to describe. From the moment that his fellow citizens called upon the rustler he was the very center of the festivity. In fact, all eyes were upon him. For once he was the observed of all observers.

He was speedily conducted to a remote region where the trees grew tall. There being few stores in the region and neckties being hard to procure, an inch rope served instead. The offending rustler was soon given a commanding position above the rest of the company and the party broke up feeling well satisfied because there was one less cattle thief in the world. Of course this was not lawful, but it was a sort of primitive justice.

Not only did the cattle men have to contend with the rustlers but soon very serious differences sprang up between themselves. These were over grazing grounds, water holes, and priority of brands, etc. Here again there were no courts to settle these disputes and once again primitive methods were resorted to.

These cattle feuds became so bad in portions of Texas and New Mexico and even farther north that as a result many scores of cow-punchers finally left their bones bleaching in the sun upon the mesas and tablelands as a result of these disputes. The arbitor in most cases was the renowned Colt's forty-five revolver which the cow-puncher always carried in the holster upon his thigh.

As soon as the homesteaders flocked into the grazing country and began building homes and tilling the land, another quarrel arose.   This w?s between the settler, or nester, as he was often called and the cattle men. These nesters often preempted the water holes which were very important and also fenced off the best grazing lands, so pitched battles ensued between the cattle men and the settlers who were frequently of foreign birth and unacquainted with our laws and customs.

About 1892 this tension between the homesteaders and the cattle kings came to a crisis.   This was when the cow-punchers assembled two hundred strong, and tried to dispel a settler from his holding in which he had fenced off the best water hole in the region.   This force of cattle men were promptly met by an equal body of local deputies which was largely made up of homesteaders.   A pitched battle was imminent near Cheyenne, Wyoming, when the United States cavalry appeared, and dispersed both parties, and the despotic power of the cattle men was forever broken.   After that, barbed wire fences appeared on many of the great ranches and the cattle business was restricted.

Then there were still other fights between the cattle men and the sheep men, and finally the goat men appeared and cleaned up what the sheep had left. So from the time when the first herds of domestic cattle appeared upon the western prairies the cattle business has been surrounded by romance and glamour, and attended with fighting and many conditions that lent themselves to dramatic action.

The cowboy from the very early days has been a picturesque historic figure, figuring very largely in the literature of the great west. In the very early days his life was a hard one, and many have been the stirring scenes in which he has taken part. He has ranged all the way from the Rio Grande on the south, to the Peace River in the very northern confines of civilization in British America. The cow-puncher also has ridden over the great divide into California, and up into Oregon and Washington. But wherever he has gone he has always been a chivalrous hero doing his work like a man. He might well be called the knight of the plains.

He has always ridden his faithful broncho, or mustang, or cayuse, according to the locality where his range was located. But by all three names this is still the same wirey, devil-may-care, little horse, tough as a pine knot, and doing a day's work that would kill any other horse in the world.

The cowboy's dress had been as picturesque as his wild life, with the broad-brimmed felt hat, the bright kerchief, the oil slicker worn in stormy weather, and the tall riding boots and chaps not to mention the historic forty-five reposing in the holster on his hip.

All these are well known characteristics of this knight of the plains.

There are few dull days in the life of a cow-puncher for adventure camps upon his trail, so what with heading off wild stampedes of cattle on dark nights, riding at a headlong pace, God only knows just where, and fighting cattle rustlers and nesters, as well as wolves and grizzly bears, the cow-puncher has always had plenty to test his nerve and keep him fit.

In the old days of the Gilson and Santa Fe trails the cattle used to be driven to the north in the summer time and back south in the winter migrating just as the buffalo did. But today all the large open ranges are gone. Instead the cattle graze over a much smaller range and the riding is all done from a central camp in one day.

All these things have tended to narrow down the once endless range of possibilities in the cowboy's life, so that to-day he is a much more sophisticated creature than of yore. And cannot expect a skulking Indian to take a pot shot at him as he rides over the range, while the grizzly has become much more wary and fearful of repeating rifles.

So with this word picture of the cowboy's arena and the conditions and action which have given him his place in both fiction and history, I leave you to the adventures of this knight of the range, and more especially to the heroism of his faithful little horse. He may on occasion buck like a fractious ram and try to pile his rider in a sorry heap on the ground, but when his antics are over he will carry his rider at a pace which would leave the best cavalry horses dead on the trail at the end of twenty-four hours. For this wild horse is a product of nature, toughened by exposure and hard conditions, and he has the fiber and heart of a wind-whipped oak.

PATCHES

THE KILLER REARED UPON HIS HIND LEGS

CHAPTER I

A RUNNING FIGHT

HANK BRODIE sat easily in his saddle on his favorite mount, Old Baldy, gazing with a rapt expression at the sun-kissed peaks of the distant mountains. It was a scene that he had beheld hundreds of times before in the course of fifteen years upon

21

Crooked Creek ranch, but somehow this scene always drew him with a strange power. It was as though a great hand had been stretched out and with unseen fingers played upon the harp strings of his being sweet low music, for Hank was a dreamer and a poet as well as a cow-puncher.

Of course his name was Henry, but if you had called him that to any of his cow-puncher pals, they would have looked at you quizzically and then replied, "Beggin' your pardon, stranger, we calls him Hank in these here parts."

He was the typical cowboy figure, lean and muscular, and with muscles like rawhide even like the rawhide lariat which he carried by his side. He was quick and alert either with the rope or the six shot Colt's revolver which reposed in the holster on his right hip. His dress was the usual cow-puncher outfit, with the broad brimmed gray felt Stetson, and the bright kerchief about his neck. This handkerchief had a dual usage. It was either a neck piece or mask as occasion required. You may wonder where he would use a disguise, but there were several occasions in the cattleman's warfare with cattle rustlers and homesteaders where a mask might be convenient. Hank wore no coat and his vest was usually unbuttoned, showing the flannel outing shirt underneath. The nearest approach to a coat he had was the slicker which he carried on the back of his saddle.

His riding breeches were just ordinary pants supplemented by ornamental chaps, but his long-legged boots were quite exceptional, with their tall slim heels and their thin soles. The tall heels were to keep the foot from catching in the stirrups and the thin soles to enable the rider to better feel the stirrup. In the pockets of his vest he always carried matches and Durham tobacco cigarettes.

For training and life background Hank was not the usual puncher, for he had been born in the east and had seen two years at Harvard University. Because of this background his fellow punchers sometimes called him Doc, but he was a thorough cattle man for all that.

For the past three days he had been out on what he termed a "fool chase." He was looking for a blooded mare named Kentucky Bell, the property of the Crooked Creek ranch owner. This fine mare had been lured away the summer before by some one of the outlaw mustang stallions that sometimes came through the mountains to the west and frequented the range, in fact she had been seen recently consorting with a notorious outlaw stallion known as the Black Killer and Mr. Morgan, the manager, was most anxious to recover her.

The Black Killer was a devilish outlaw mustang who had killed more than one man and several domestic horses on the ranches. He was only an occasional visitor to the Crooked Creek ranch, but even so he was a menace to both man and beast. There is among the wild horses one out of a thousand, or perhaps ten thousand, known as a killer. They are the most dangerous animal upon the western ranges, more cunning than any bear or wolf and much more to be feared.

Such a horse will often permit himself to be caught along with a score of other wild horses, and never show the killing tendency until he gets his prey at his mercy and then he strikes like lightning. The cow-puncher's mount is much quicker to sense the presence of a killer than is his rider, so when a horse begins to champ his bit nervously and to drool with excitement and fear and draw away from an unseen danger, the cow-puncher always reaches for his trusty six shooter.

Hank had told Mr. Morgan that it was like looking for a needle in a haymow to try to find the mare on the range of several hundred thousand acres and as for the Black Killer he was more wary than a grizzly, but Mr. Morgan had insisted and Hank had gone on this "wild goose chase" as he styled it.

Obedience is one of the ranch's first laws and Hank, as the head cow-puncher, had to obey. So, for the past three days he and Baldy had been scouring the country, but had not seen a sign of either the mare or the killer.

Hank was so engrossed with his day dream of watching the sunset that his usually alert senses were for the moment off guard, so it was Old Baldy who first discovered that all was not well in the landscape about them, for without a moment's warning he threw up his head and snorted and then pulled restively at the bit.

"Whoa, whoa, old scout," said Hank soothingly. "What is it, old chap?"

Again Baldy snorted and pulled at the bit. He had either heard or scented something that his master had missed. What in the dickens could it be? But Hank was immediately informed, for a terrified, agonized squeal from a horse in distress cut the stillness like a knife. It was some distance away, but there was no mistaking the sound.

Hank turned partly around in his saddle and looked up the canyon behind them. Baldy had been standing where a branch creek emptied into Crooked Creek. In midsummer this small creek would be entirely dry, but now there was a little water in the river bed. What Hank saw filled him with astonishment and anxiety, for the objects of his double quest were in full sight, about an eighth of a mile up the canyon where it narrowed down between the walls.

A small colt perhaps two months old was in the foreground. He was running like a jackrabbit and his mother, who was none other than Kentucky Bell, was following close behind him trying desperately to ward off the fiendish effort of a coal black stallion who was springing and biting at the colt with deadly intent. The mare was putting up a desperate running fight, but the colt seemed doomed although he ran like an antelope and doubled and twisted as the old fury came close to him.

Now the ill fame of the killer had travelled all over that portion of the state. There was not a cow-puncher in the region that had not much rather meet a grizzly bear than the killer, but his duty was plain so Hank reined 'Baldy sharply about and galloped rapidly towards that desperate running fight. He knew full well that he ran some risk in so doing, but a cowboy's life is full of adventure and he was enured to danger of every sort.

Again and again the little horse seemed lost, for the black stallion would swoop down upon him, his teeth snapping like a bear trap, but just in time the colt would jump aside or the mare would intervene, receiving ugly bites herself.

So intent was the killer with the object in view that

he did not notice Hank and Old Baldy until they were about fifty yards away. Then he spotted them and immediately the colt was forgotten and the black fury charged straight down the canyon at this new foe. The battle would have been a short one but for the nervousness of Baldy who sensed even more fully than his master the deadly character of the oncoming horse.

Hank had just raised his Colt's to shoot when the sight of the charging fury overwhelmed Baldy and he wheeled like a flash and galloped towards Crooked Creek while the bullet which would certainly have struck the stallion went whizzing over his head.

Hank sawed away upon the bit and did his best to quiet Baldy, but his panic was complete, so the best Hank could do was to fire over his shoulder at his pursuer. This was at best very inaccurate shooting and he saw his revolver being rapidly emptied to no purpose.

If he could only stop Baldy long enough for a good shot he would at least wound the fury, but Baldy had no mind to come to grips with this black devil.

Closer and closer the fury came. Baldy could probably have run away from him had Hank plied the quirt, but he had no such intentions so he and his mount were working at cross purposes. When they reached Crooked Creek, Hank guided Baldy down stream where the bank was smooth and finally after desperate sawing upon the bit managed to bring him to a partial stop for just a second. Just long enough to turn in the saddle and get a good shot. At the crack of the revolver Hank heard the stallion squeal. He had scored. But to his great surprise the outlaw turned and disappeared among some piñons to the south and Hank saw no more of him.

The cow-puncher now had time to reload his revolver, for this good shot had been his last cartridge, and keeping a good sharp watch for the stallion, he went to look for the mare and colt.

He found Kentucky Bell near the spot where he had last seen her, and she seemed glad to see him and allowed herself to be roped without much difficulty.

The colt who had been badly scared by the outlaw was at first rather shy, but it kept close to the mare's flank and when Hank started on the long journey to the ranch house the colt followed obediently.

Half a mile up the creek it occurred to Hank that he should not have let the outlaw get away so easily, so after some deliberation he hitched the mare securely to a small piñon and went back to look for the Black Killer. He had now accomplished half the object of his quest and he wished to accomplish the other half.

He scoured the canyon, where he had last seen him, for an hour, but could not get a sight of him. Finally, as it was getting late in the afternoon, Hank retraced his steps, back to the colt and mare.

He had hidden them in a narrow draw and at first he thought he had not remembered the place rightly, for the mare did not seem to be where he had left her. Finally after some searching he found the identical piñon to which he had tied the mare, but she was gone.

Yet, that was not all, the tree was broken down and there were signs of a desperate struggle. With a sense of foreboding Hank began searching the draw and soon came upon the mare. She was quite dead and the colt was nowhere to be seen.

Then the full purport of the tragedy came home to Hank. The old outlaw had been following him at a distance all the time. He had followed just as a grizzly will sometimes trail a man and when he was out of sight he had fallen upon the helpless mare. She had broken away in the course of the struggle, but had finally been killed.

At the sight of the broken bushes and trampled ferns Hank looked at his six gun to see that every chamber was full and that it was in readiness. They were not done with this business yet. As he hurried back to Baldy whom he had tied near that fatal piñon, he was aroused to a new danger by seeing Baldy pulling at his picket line. Then Baldy broke away and galloped madly towards the creek leaving Hank alone in the draw.

"Well, I guess the devil is somewhere near," thought Hank. "Baldy wouldn't have bolted like that unless the old Satan was snooking about. I guess I am in for it now."

Baldy's hoof beats had barely died away when other hoofs were heard and the killer trotted out of the draw from a clump of cedars where he had been hiding all the time.

Hank's first impulse was to run for a small tree nearby or to climb to the top of a pile of boulders fifty feet away, but he had hardly time for either maneuver for the fury charged upon him like a cyclone, snapping his teeth and raging like a veritable demon.

Then the words of Colonel Roosevelt came to Hank and they helped to steady his hand and steel his heart. "If any wild animal ever charges you, do not run away, but stand perfectly still and keep shooting. There is not an animal living that can kill a man if he keeps his nerve."

Well, Hank would do just that. There was no other alternative. When the fury was sixty feet away the six shooter cracked for the first shot and a wisp of the black horse's mane dropped to the ground. The wound was a bad one in the neck, but not fatal and the killer went mad at the pain. After that he did not mind bullets or pain. His only object was to get at his foe. Twice the revolver cracked again before he had covered half the remaining distance. Each time he was badly wounded, but thus far Hank had not hit a vital spot.

Then the killer did a foolish thing for he reared upon his hind legs and walked forward, striking with his forefeet and gnashing his teeth. Hank afterward said it was the most terrifying sight he had ever seen. To miss now was sure death, but the stallion had made the wrong move for this maneuver slowed up his charge and the cowboy sent two shots into his body and one into his head, and with a last desperate effort the killer charged forward and fell dead almost at Hank's feet. Coolness and the good Colt's revolver had won.

The stallion had barely ceased to struggle and Hank had hardly recovered from the great excitement of the few dramatic moments when he was treated to another surprise for his attention was attracted by some moving object at the very top of the pile of stones where he had thought of taking refuge when the stallion charged.

His first thought was that it was a skulking coyote, but on circling about the pile of stones he soon discovered that it was a small colt, and as he climbed up close to the terrified little horse he saw to his great surprise that it was Kentucky Bell's foal, the very one that the old killer had been trying to destroy when he had first caught sight of them.

The colt was very fearful of the cow-puncher, but he was perched up so high that he did not dare jump and Hank had purposely cut off the only good way of descent. So Hank got his rope which fortunately he had thrown on the ground when he hitched Baldy and lassoed the small horse and brought him plunging and very much afraid to the level ground. But now that he had him safely down, Hank was in a quandary to know how to get the colt home. Mr. Morgan, he knew, would never forgive him if he abandoned the colt now. So with great patience the cow-puncher started to halter break the colt to see if he would lead.

The small horse acted just like all colts and immediately sulked and threw himself and had to be dragged to his feet. Finally after an hour's hard work Hank got the colt so he would stand and not pull on the rope, but he did not think he would lead. In fact, as soon as he had secured Baldy and mounted and pulled on the rope, the colt again flopped to the ground. Finally the cow-puncher bound his legs with some thongs with which his saddle bags were always generously supplied and threw him across the saddle just as he would have done a dead deer and started to walk the five miles to Crooked Creek ranch. He stopped several times to change the position of the colt and to readjust the slicker and piñon boughs under him. The colt thought his lot was very hard, judging from his sighs and occasional groans, but Hank assured him it was much better than being eaten up by the stallion.

About nine o'clock that night the cow-puncher arrived at the ranch, footsore and tired, but well pleased with his part in the expedition. For he had killed the killer and earned the reward of five hundred dollars, and had also rescued Kentucky Bell's colt which Mr. Morgan would prize very highly. It was an exploit that would give the cow-puncher something to talk about for several days so Hank was well pleased with the outcome.

CHAPTER II

THE TENDERFOOT

FOUR years have now elapsed since that eventful day when Hank Brodie had engaged in that desperate running fight with the Killer, in which through sheer pluck and good shooting he had saved the life of Kentucky Bell's little colt. If one had seen that small horse lashed to Hank's saddle as he toted him home, and could also have seen the eleven hundred pound gelding which now pranced about over the ranch, free as the winds that blew, it would have been another striking reminder of the adage, "Great oaks from little acorns grow."

Never since that day when Hank had unbound the small horse and set him upon his feet before the ranch corral had he been haltered or bridled. A ranch mare which had lost her own colt the day before, had at once adopted the forlorn little horse and everything had gone on just as though he had not lost his own mother.

It is general practice among ranchmen not to break a colt until he is four years old, when he is supposed to have reached his full size and strength. Even the breaking that he gets is not the long painstaking course

34

of lessons which an eastern horse gets, but a rather harsh course of object lessons, in which he has to learn, or suffer the consequences. His breaking is always with force and this is force spelt with a capital F. Horses are plenty and cheap upon the western ranches, and time is valuable, so a man cannot spend too much time fussing with a refractory broncho. But most of these wild horses, which in some cases have been crossed with native stock, are very clever, and they learn rapidly, so after several severe lessons they are ready to ride, all but the outlaw, who is never safe or sure.

This refractory animal is naturally full of cussedness, and he may be expected to buck, kick, and bite at any time during his stormy life.

He is usually upon the bad string in the corral, and ultimately finds himself doing bucking stunts at the famous round-ups, or Rodeos which the cowboys hold each autumn at several western centres.

At these spectacular shows there is a premium upon pure cussedness so even the outlaw finds his place in the economy of the cattle country.

It had been as cold and blustery a Spring day as had come to the Wyoming foot-hills in many a year; a day of scudding white clouds and rapidly moving shadows; a day that made one turn up his coat collar and seek shelter if possible.

Now in the early evening the boisterous north wind was holding high carnival about the ranch house and the out-buildings of the Crooked Creek ranch. He was picking up pieces of old paper, bits of twigs and last year's dead leaves and tossing them about in high glee. The scudding wind clouds partially hid the moon and the stars. Few sounds could be heard above the howling of the wind, only the shrill, tremulous whistle of a screech owl and the diabolical yapping of a pair of coyotes.

If it was cold and blustery outside, warmth and comfort reigned inside the ranch house. The long low room was bright with the light of two lamps and a great log fire which crackled and danced in the huge fire-place. By the long table were seated fourteen cow-punchers, hale and hearty boys and the working force of the Crooked Creek ranch.

At the head of the table sat Mr. Morgan, superintendent of the ranch. At his right was Hank Brodie, the head cow-puncher, and near him his nephew, young Larry Winton, who had come up from Terryville that very afternoon. He had made the trip on a buckboard with his trunk, which contained all his worldly possessions, lashed on behind.

Larry was Hank Brodie's only near relative. His mother had been Hank's only sister, but she had died two weeks before, and as the boy's father had died

"MEBBE HE WAS THINKING OF SAW HORSES"

when he was a mere child, this had left him homeless.
He was also nearly penniless and the invitation from
his uncle in the Wyoming hills to come and live with
him had been gladly accepted. Larry had dreamed
of finishing high school and going to college but since
he had no money and few friends in the East, he tem-
porarily gave up the idea of school and went West.

The West had always had a strong appeal for him.
The broad spaces and adventurous life of which he had

read in books had kindled his imagination so he had entered upon this new adventure with great zest.

He was a tall athletic youth, five feet, ten inches in height and weighing one hundred fifty-five pounds, although he was not quite sixteen years of age. He was muscular and athletic. He had always played base-ball and football and camped and tramped, in fact he was a fine product of that great organization, the Boy Scouts. As he sat by his uncle's side looking at the jolly company around the table he wondered what they would think of him. They certainly were a hearty looking company. He had never seen food disappear so fast before. Mrs. Morgan, the wife of the superin-tendent, and Olga, the Swedish maid, had all they could do to keep the plates well-filled. Such simple fare as potatoes, which the cow-punchers always call spuds, bacon and eggs, brown bread, coffee, and pumpkin pie were disappearing at an alarming rate.

If Larry was curious about the cow-punchers, they were also curious about this young tenderfoot who had just arrived from the East and they immediately began feeling him out in a jovial good-natured manner.

If the cow-punchers were inclined to tease, Larry's Uncle Henry would not interfere for he wanted his nephew to be at once put upon his mettle and to start the new life aright.

"Your Uncle Hank says you can ride," said Big

Bill, turning to Larry during a pause in the conversation.

"Why, yes," said Larry, eager to get into their good graces. "Major Winterby, our riding master, says I can ride anything that stands on four legs."

The moment the words were out of his mouth he regretted such a sweeping assertion, but every cowpuncher at the table immediately drew on his poker face. This was a serious, non-committal expression as blank as a bare wall, but if Larry had known, they exchanged sly pokes under the table.

"He wasn't a-referring to feather beds or rocking chairs, was he?" put in Long Tom.

"Mebbe he was thinking of saw-horses," interjected Pony Perkins.

At these sallies Larry grew hot with indignation, but at a warning look from his uncle he returned a good-natured answer, "Well, gentlemen, perhaps I did overstate it."

"Here, here, kid," called an old cow-puncher from across the table, "don't you gentlemen us. We don't have any sech out here in the Wyoming hills. We are all gents. If you call a chap a gentlemen out here, that is next to calling him a hoss thief, a cattle rustler, or a gambler who don't pay his bills. Gentlemen is a fighting word out here and it usually precedes bullets."

"Excuse me, gentlemen, I mean gents," corrected Larry. "You see I don't know your customs and I will have to learn them."

"Why, of course," put in Big Bill, "you will learn in no time. We are kind of different out here, we has our ways and we sticks by them."

"What kind of hosses did this air major of your'n ride," inquired Texas Pete. "Was they bronchos or was they high-bred stock?"

"They surely were not bronchos," replied Larry. "The most of them were saddle horses, but some were polo ponies and they were often good jumpers. Major Winterby usually got first prize at the great Eastern States Exposition."

"How high could one of them fancy hosses jump?" asked Long Tom. "I've seen some high jumping myself among the wild hosses."

"I think the Major's record with Comet was seven feet, four inches."

At this announcement a low whistle escaped several of the cowboys and Larry followed up this good impression.

"But the world's record is eight feet, six inches," he continued.

"Well," said Pony Perkins, "that's some jump but I've seen one of the fuzzy tails beat that. One time me and Arizona Tom was up in the big Pine River country catching fuzzy tails. We built a big trap around a water-hole and Tom and me hid in a pit nearby to watch it. We watched for two nights and nothing came along. Then a big bunch of fuzzy tails went into our trap and we sprung the trigger. One of them was a black stallion, the finest wild hoss I ever saw. He ran around the enclosure for a minute or two, then going to one side of it, he took two quick jumps and then a big spring and went over the top slick as a sliver. I jumped on my hoss and put after him but he was out of sight in two shakes of a lamb's tail, making about fourteen feet at a stride. When I measured that fence, it was nine feet high."

"Well," said Larry, "I guess that beats the world's record for high jumping, but you must remember that those horses jumped with a man on their back while this horse was riderless."

"That's true," said Pony.

"How are your Eastern saddles rigged," inquired Big Bill. "Are they single shot or double shot?"

Larry looked inquiringly at his uncle. "He means, are they rigged with one cinch or two."

"That's still dark to me," said Larry. "I don't even know what a cinch is."

"That isn't strange," said his uncle, "here we say cinches, but in the East we say saddle girt."

"Oh," said Larry, "We have one girt."

"Single shot," chorused the cow-punchers.

"Be they center fire or three quarters rigged?" inquired Long Tom.

"That's another on me," said Larry.

"I see I shall have to explain again," said Uncle Henry. "On our Western saddles we have two straps coming down from the tree. At the angle where they meet there is a ring and the cinch is lashed into that ring. If these straps are of equal length it is center fire, but if the forward one is shorter than the other it is three quarters."

"I see," said Larry, "we have one strap coming down from the saddle tree."

"I dunno," said Long Tom, "but I'm afeared that a single rigged wouldn't hold a thousand pound steer when you brung him up short. I'm afeared you would lose steer, rider, and saddle."

"I am wondering," put in Pony Perkins, "what your Major would think if he was on a wild hoss, one that would crowhop, and sunfish, and swap ends. I guess he would think there was something doing."

"Perhaps he would," said Larry, "but he is a good hurdle rider and a fine polo player."

"That air polo game is some game," said Big Bill. "Me and California Joe usen to play it for the moving picter folks down at Los Angeles."

"That's so," said Long Tom. "Why, Big Bill's middle name is polo."

"That's fine," said Larry. "We will have to have a team this summer."

This suggestion was received with great enthusiasm and they entered into a discussion of the game of polo with much zest.

By this time the table had been cleared off and the men had pushed back their chairs and many of them had lit their cigarettes. But Pony Perkins had gone over to one of the windows where he stood looking out into the darkness. Noticing Pony's posture and his quiet manner a hush had fallen over the cowboys. Big Bill leaned over to Larry and whispered, "You jest watch Pony. I s'pect he will break forth in a minute. He has got a touch of religion coming on. He experienced religion down at a camp meeting at Wyanne last summer."

Larry looked over his shoulder at Pony. He was a small man and his attitude indicated deep concentration. Presently he turned and faced his fellow cowboys. His face was bright with a wonderful smile and his eyes had a gleam in them like the light of the stars.

"Gents," he said, raising his right hand for silence, "I feel the spirit of the Lord acoming down out of Heaven upon me. Yes, I feel it acoming, gents, and it is like Chinook, the south wind, when he breathes over the brown ranches in the Spring. For the spirit of the Lord is full of life and gentleness and it is acoming to me, gents."

"I see the Lord acoming down from Heaven on a white hoss. He is agalloping on the clouds. On His saddle horn is a new rope and He is acoming to rope all you onery old steers. Now, gents, when the Lord rides by don't put down your heads and paw the dirt, and bellow, and kick up a fuss. But jest hold up your heads and let the Lord rope ye. Then when He has roped ye, He will get out His branding iron and put His name on your foreheads and you will be His'n forever. Hallelujah, I see the Lord acoming. He is looking for all His onery old ranch steers, and all the cattle hear His voice and they are acoming. Down from the broad plateau they are acoming, from the high mesa they are acoming, from the deep canyons they are acoming, rejoicing at the call of the Lord. And, gents, you may think the Lord is fer off but He is right here among us jest ropin' cow-punchers. It won't be so long until the great round-up, the day when the Lord drives us all home on the Heavenly trail to live forever in His green pasture. And, oh, cowboys, the feed will be sweet on the Lord's ranch and the pools of water will be so fresh that when you have drunk of them you never will be thirsty again. O, cow-punchers, make ready, tighten up your belts and be smiling when the Lord comes."

As Pony finished it was so still in the room that one could have heard a pin drop. The cow-punchers who had been grinning when he began were all looking solemn. Long Tom had copied Pony's heavenly smile and Big Bill was surreptitiously wiping away tears.

"That's some sermon, Pony," said Big Bill.

"You gin it to us good," ejaculated Long Tom.

"That was fine, Pony," said Mr. Morgan. "I guess we all know what you meant and I can see the boys all took it to heart."

"Now, gents," continued Pony, "don't you fellers get to thinking that I am spouting jest to hear myself spout. I couldn't help it; it was the spirit of the Lord came down on me and I jest bust out like a geyser. Now, gents, let us all conclude this evening by singing the cow-puncher's hymn, When We Are Rounded Up in Glory."

They began the old cowboy hymn rather quietly, but the verses gathered volume as they went on until finally they were singing at the top of their voices and the rafters of the low room fairly rang. Presently they were swinging to and fro and keeping time upon the table with their fists or stamping their feet. It was a great religious marching song, Rounded Up In Glory, for every man at the rude table entered into it with all his soul.

When the sound of the last vigorous verse had died away, the company slowly dispersed and the cow-punchers made their way to the bunk house, two or three of the older men stopping to slap Pony on the back and to tell him that he was a good old sky pilot and they would rather hear him preach than any of the sky pilots down at Wyanne.

The bunk house was very much like the ranch house in construction, a long low building with a row of army cots on either side and an aisle in the middle. At the head of each cot was a chair that had seen better days.

Laughing and joking about the weather and the day's work ahead, the cow-punchers stripped off coats, breeches, and chaps and piled them upon the chairs and stood their tall boots by the cots, then shot into their cots like prairie dogs into their holes. In five minutes time the entire company were between the sheets.

It seemed to Larry that the men fell asleep as soon as their heads touched the pillows, for soon nearly the entire crowd was snoring prodigiously. It seemed to the young tenderfoot that he had never heard such snores before.

He lay awake for several minutes listening to the

sleeping men and the howling wind outside with an
occasional whistle from a screech owl or a howl from
a coyote. Then he, too, fell asleep and dreamed of
the Lord coming down from Heaven on a white horse,
coming for the great round-up to bring home his cow-
punchers to the Heavenly ranch to be with Him forever.

THE WEST ALWAYS HAD A STRONG APPEAL FOR LARRY

CHAPTER III

THE SPRING ROUND-UP

FULLY an hour before daylight the following morning Larry was awakened by the cowboys who were up and dressing. The clothes they had thrown upon the chairs so unceremoniously the night before, were as hastily donned by the feeble light of a kerosene lamp and they were ready for the day's work.

"Gracious," ejaculated Larry, jumping out of bed, "do we have to work in the dark out here on the ranch?"

"No, not exactly," said Uncle Henry, "but you see this is the first day of the Spring round-up. It is always a hard day and we like to get an early start. There is nothing like starting the day right. You wait a minute, Larry, I've got some cowboy togs for you."

He went to a large closet at the end of the bunk house and brought out a brand new suit, Stetson, kerchief, chaps, tall boots, and all.

"What, are those for me, Uncle?" cried the boy, delightedly.

48

"Yes," said Mr. Brodie, "I sent down to Wyanne and got them for you just as soon as I received your letter saying you were coming. I want you to be a real cow-puncher from the start. You are going with the round-up men today. I am going to let you ride Old Dobbin. He is a native horse and doesn't know what the word buck means, besides he isn't old either."

Presently Larry found himself seated once more at the long table in the ranch house where several platters of hot sourdough griddle cakes were waiting the cow-punchers. These, with bacon and hot coffee and plenty of maple syrup and butter, were the regulation morning meal at the ranch house. A big crock behind the kitchen stove was always filled with the sourdough.

The morning meal was not eaten as leisurely as supper had been. This was the beginning of the day's work and the cow-punchers went at it in a businesslike manner. Soon the griddle cakes and bacon were dispatched and all were off to the corral for their ponies.

To lasso one's favorite pony in the corral with a hundred others, all moving about and restless, was not an easy matter, but to do this in semi-darkness and with the ponies ducking to escape the flying nooses was quite a difficult matter. But one by one the ponies were secured and brought outside the corral; then began the process of saddling and bridling.

"What, haven't those horses even been broken?" asked Larry of his uncle in surprise, as the horses pirouetted and snorted and jumped about when the men sought to saddle them.   One pony even had to be thrown and his legs hobbled before the cow-puncher could get him saddled.

"Why, sure," returned Mr. Brodie, "most of these are seasoned horses, but they have been running on the range all winter and haven't been worked, so on a morning like this they are full of kinks and have to work off their steam somehow."

If Larry had been surprised at the trouble in saddling the bronchos, he was still more surprised when the first one mounted began to buck. He would put his head down between his knees and then buck straight into the air, three or four feet, and come down stiff-legged giving his rider a terrific jolt.

"Gracious," ejaculated Larry, "I wouldn't want to be on that piece of horse flesh.   What is the matter with him?   Is he ugly?"

"Oh, no," returned Uncle Henry, "he is just working off steam.   We always say that a mustang that won't buck is bad in some other way. We like to have them buck, then we know they're natural.   I had a broncho once that never bucked until I had ridden him a year and then he tried to slam me into the corral fence and kill me. He nearly broke his own neck and would have broken mine as well if I hadn't slid out of the saddle. Then he 'broke wide open' as we say and the cussedness which he should have worked off a little at a time, came all at once, so in the slang of the cattle land 'let 'em buck'."

When Old Dobbin, as he was called, was brought out Larry was surprised to see a handsome Iowa horse of about ten hundred pounds.

"He's as clever as the day is long," remarked Uncle Henry, as they swung into their saddles, "and he knows the cattle game almost as well as the bronchoes. You just give him his head most of the time and he'll do the rest."

So they galloped after the cow-punchers and the first day of the Spring round-up begun.

"You see," explained Mr. Brodie, riding up close to his nephew, "this Spring round-up used to be a complicated affair before the ranches were all fenced. No one could brand even his own cattle until the day of the round-up was appointed by the superintendent of each district. Then the cow-punchers of several ranches all got together and drove the cattle to one place where they were branded and sorted out by the inspector, with a bookkeeper to note down the stock which belonged to each ranch. The branding practise

is an old one. The first branding irons were brought
from Spain by Cortez and Pizarro. Cattle have always
been branded in Spain. We also got our first long-
horned stock from the Mexicans, but now it has been
bred out, and most of our herds are short-horned
Durham and Hereford."

"Where are we headed for?" asked Larry.

"Ultimately we are going to Piñon Valley. This
ranch happens to be beautifully located for the round-
up. At this time of year all of the cattle are on the
lower plateau because the feed is better there. So we
cut out a thousand head a day and run them into
Piñon Valley and there we hold them until we have
branded all the calves and the cows that need it. Then
we feed them in through what we call the neck of the
bottle that leads to the upper plateau. It takes about
ten days to put the entire herd through this process."

When Uncle Henry and Larry arrived at Piñon
Valley they found small groups of cattle already streaming into the lower end for the cow-punchers had preceded Larry and his uncle by half an hour. Larry
saw that Piñon Valley was about three hundred yards
long and one hundred yards wide. The sides of the
valley were very precipitate and covered with piñons
and junipers. Three cow-punchers had been placed
at the head of the valley to keep the cattle from going
through to the upper plateau. Larry and his uncle

WITH A SHARP PULL ON THE REINS, HE WHEELED BALDY TO THE LEFT

sat on their horses and watched the cattle come into the valley. It was a wonderful sight. To Larry they seemed endless.

"My," he said, "what a herd."

"That's only a fragment," returned Uncle Henry, "some day I will take you to a nearby hill where we can see most of the herd through a field glass. That will be a sight worth seeing."

"What is that pink streak way off to the East?" asked Larry.

"I was wondering if you would notice it," returned his uncle. "That is man's reward for getting up early. It is the miracle of the new day. Old Sol is just climbing up over the Sierras. It's a sight to set one right for the entire day. Just watch it, boy."

Larry watched and the pink streak which at first had been small grew in both width and length and also in brightness. The pink became red and then the red was suffused with an unearthly radiance. The snow on the distant mountain tops refracted the sunlight till all the colors of the prism showed. With each passing second the glory grew in brightness until old Sol finally burst into full view, the center of all this splendor.

"My," exclaimed Larry, "it takes one's breath away."

"You bet," returned Uncle Henry. "This is a great country. It's a great place for a young man to grow up in, the wide spaces, bracing air, and the blue sky are good for a man's soul."

"What do you say, Mr. Brodie," cried a cow-puncher, riding up, "have we got enough?" The head cow-puncher looked over the seething mass of cattle in Piñon Valley with an appraising eye, then said, "All right, shut down the gate."

Then a dozen cow-punchers, including Mr. Brodie
and Larry, made a cordon across the lower end of
Piñon Valley and the main herd were turned back.
When the imprisoned cattle had begun to quiet down
and the steers had worked their way to the center of
the herd as they always do on such an occasion, the
branding began. Soon little fires were seen all about
the perimeter of the valley. Presently the cowboys
began roping calves. It seemed to Larry like a rather
brutal process.

The rope would whiz through the air and fall over a
calf's head, then if he were not near enough to the fire
for the brand to be applied, he would be dragged unceremoniously into the proper position. Then the branding iron, which was six inches broad and seven inches
long, would be thrust against his rump. It did not
matter if he thrashed, or kicked, or bleated, the branding process went on. When the hair had been entirely singed off and the trade mark of the Crooked
Creek Cattle Company burned into his skin, he was
loosed and allowed to go to his excited mother. The
brand for this particular ranch was C C R with a strand
of barbed wire above and beneath, and also at either
end.

"You see," explained Uncle Henry, "we have to make
the brand more or less complicated, just C C R would

not do for some rustler would come along and close up the two C's and then it would read O O R."

"Is that ever done?" inquired Larry.

"Oh, yes," replied his uncle. "The rustler's game is really a very serious menace to the cattle business. In the old days the ranchers used to lose more cattle from rustling than from any other cause. We have to be very careful in selecting the brand."

"How do you keep from getting the same brand?" inquired Larry.

"Well, you see, it is this way, the branding irons are all registered at the county seat. They have to be registered just as a trade mark is patented and the registrar sees to it that no branding iron is duplicated."

Soon Larry's attention was attracted by a cow which objected seriously to having her calf branded. Finally she charged the cow-puncher with the rope so viciously that he had to call another herdsman to rope the cow and hold her while they branded the calf. Soon the air, which had been sweet with the breath of the morning wind when they had first come to Piñon Valley, was filled with the smell of singeing hair and burning flesh, and the steam and reek of a thousand excited cattle. Hour after hour the work went on, cutting out cows and calves, branding the helpless little calves and then driving them forward to the head of Piñon Valley where they were in turn driven through the cul de sac

or neck of the bottle to the upper plateau. At noon
the chuck wagon came up and the cow-punchers by
relays ate a hasty lunch.

"You see," explained Uncle Henry, "the chuck
wagon has about gone out of business. In the old days
when the cattle were often driven even hundreds of
miles from the home ranch, the chuck wagon followed
after them and the cowboys lived in the open. But
today it is what we call a one day stand, that is, most
of the riding is done from the home ranch and we
can reach any point on the ranch between sunup and
sundown."

Soon the cow-punchers were back at their gruesome
work.

"I don't see how they manage to go 'way into the
center of the herd and get the cows and calves as they
do. The pony also seems to know which cow they are
after," said Larry.

"That is one of the mysteries of the cattle game," explained his uncle, "the intelligence of some of these
cow-ponies. Almost as soon as you spot your cow, no
matter where it is, the pony seems to know which one
you have picked out and is after it. He is so eager
that sometimes, when a cow does not start as quickly
as he thinks she ought, he gives her a nip behind."

Feverishly the cow-punchers worked until the sun
had traveled through the high heavens and hung low

on the western Wyoming hills. They had worked fast, so when the shadows began to fall, they were able to drive the last remnant of cattle that had nearly filled Piñon Valley through the neck of the bottle to the upper plateau. Then all hands, except three who had been selected for the purpose, turned home. Those three who were left behind camped in the gorge between Piñon Valley and the upper plateau and held the branded cattle on the upper mesa. The following morning before sunup the force of the Crooked Creek ranch were off again. Once more the little valley was filled with excited, snorting, steaming cattle and once again the gruesome work of putting the Crooked Creek trade mark upon the newly-born calves began.

"See that little chap who is wandering around among the herd?" asked Uncle Henry, pointing to a small red calf. "That is a maverick, which means a calf without a mother. Either his mother was a heifer and has disowned him, or he was the smaller one of twins and got crowded out, or possibly his mother died. Anyway he is a maverick. In the old days when branding was done under inspection it was a criminal offense to brand such a calf before his ownership had been determined by the inspector."

"Is the rustling business really a serious thing now?" inquired Larry. "I have read lots about it in novels but have never felt quite sure that it was all real."

"I am sorry to say it is," returned his uncle. "There are lots of men in this world that would rather live by thieving than by getting a living honestly. The cattle business which is done on such a large scale and out in the open is especially vulnerable to such practices. It is not an unheard of thing to find your fences cut and forty or fifty fat steers missing. They always take the best ones."

"But what do they do with them?" inquired Larry.

"Why, they drive them away for a long distance and keep them for a while until the theft has been forgotten, then they sell them.

"The government has done what it could to help detect such sales for, in every county, the railroads must keep books with a list of all cattle shipped out and these figures are open for inspection any time by anybody.

"The cattle business is much more civilized today than it was twenty-five years ago, then the cattle men, the sheep men, and the goat men fought many desperate battles over the ranch land and especially the water-holes. Water, in this ranch game, is very important."

"What are the water-holes?" inquired the tenderfoot.

"You see," said his uncle, "the sub-soil in this country is clay and in all the little hollows it holds the water almost as effectively as a man-made reservoir. So, long after the spring rains have passed, water remains in these holes and the cattle come to these places to drink. It was a common thing in the old days when the cattle man had driven his herd a hundred miles to a favorite water-hole, to find it was full of drowned sheep. Even the cattle themselves sometimes push each other into the water till some are drowned.

"But the exciting thing in the cattle game in the old days was the great drive over the Santa Fe trail from New Mexico to Montana. Every spring the great herds were started from the south and driven northward for nearly a thousand miles and in the fall they were turned back southward and driven to their winter quarters. As the cowboys say, 'Them was the days'; days of rustling, of stampedes, of fights with other herdsmen, and the sheep and goat men. No cow-puncher ever complained in those days that he lacked for excitement. The days were full of it, full of excitement and danger and the hardest kind of hard work from sunup to sundown, and also through the night. For in those days they always set what they called the night watch. Then the herdsman rode round and round the cattle all night long singing his cow-puncher songs. There is something about the human voice which seems to soothe the cattle and this was the cow-puncher's easiest way to keep them quiet. Thus it is that the hundreds of cow-puncher's songs have come into existence, many of them very beautiful and full of local color."

On the tenth day after the beginning of the spring round-up, the last bunch of cattle had been driven from Piñon Valley to the upper plateau and the spring round-up was over.   This work would not be done again until September when the autumn round-up would begin.

"Now," said Uncle Henry, when the last small herd had disappeared, "I am going to take you to the top of a small mountain nearby and show you a sight which cannot be duplicated anywhere east of the Mississippi River."

So they picketed their horses and climbed up through the piñons and junipers to a small mountain.

"The piñon," said Uncle Henry, "is a small nut-bearing pine and the juniper is a small cedar.   You usually find them on very barren land."

They climbed up and up through more cedars and piñons and then through lodge-pole pines and aspens. Finally they came out into an open spot near the top of the mountain.   Larry who had thought himself a good mountain climber was in a dripping sweat.

"Now," said his uncle, taking a small field glass from his pocket, "I am going to show you one of the sights of the cattle land."   He gave Larry the glass and pointed towards the small plateau into which they had been driving the cattle for the past ten days.

Larry looked and was amazed at the sight, for as

far as he could see in every direction away to the mountains, the plateau was covered with cattle; steers, cows,
and calves, one mighty mass. He had not imagined
there were so many cattle in the entire state of
Wyoming.

He looked for at least a minute in perfect silence,
then lowered the glass. "Uncle," he said, "this is like
what it says in the Bible, 'the cattle upon a thousand
hills.'"

"I have often thought of that," returned his uncle,
"it is the fiftieth Psalm and the tenth verse, 'For every
beast of the forest is mine, and the cattle upon a thousand hills.'"

But even as they watched, the sun touched the western hill-tops and the cold night winds swept across
the mountain top. They hastened down to their ponies
and galloped home to the ranch house, for this long
low building with its dull gray exterior and its homely
outline, did really begin to seem like home to Larry. It
was always so warm and cozy inside and the cow-
punchers were such a good-natured company. They
all tried to make it pleasant for Larry and help him to
forget the recent loss of his own home in the East and
his mother.

"Ever since I came out here," said Larry to his uncle
one day, "I have been wondering why all the cow-

punchers tote a .45. So far as I can see there seems to be no use for it."

"You might think so," returned his uncle, "but it is one of the most useful aids we have on the ranch. We use it in many ways in this country. You never can tell when some danger, which has to be met with force, will sweep down on you, so one always ought to be ready."

About two weeks after this conversation Larry was riding with his uncle on the ranch when he had a very forcible demonstration of what his uncle had told him about the .45.

They had ridden clear across the big plateau to the foothills to the east when they came upon Big Bill who was out with three or four other cow-punchers inspecting the fences.

"There's a steer over here in the draw," said Bill, "which acts mighty ugly. I can't make out what is the matter with him. He seems so full of cussedness that I don't dare go very near him."

"All right," said Mr. Brodie, "let's go over and take a look at him." So he and Bill galloped away, closely followed by Larry. They soon located the steer which was a large vicious-looking animal with longer horns than most of the Crooked Creek stock.

"Looks as though he had some of the old Long Horn about him," said Bill. "He is full of gunpowder."

"Larry," said Uncle Henry, "you and old Dobbin go over there in those piñons. You keep an eye on the steer and be ready to beat it if he comes after you. Bill and I will see if we can rope him and find out what is the matter."

So the head cow-puncher and Bill approached the steer from opposite directions, each with his lariat coiled and ready. As they drew near, the steer lowered his head, pawed the ground, and bellowed almost continuously. First he would face one man, then turn and face the other. When Uncle Henry and Baldy were within about one hundred feet of him, he wheeled about and faced Bill and seemed about to charge. Then the head cow-puncher touched Baldy with the spur and galloped forward. At the same time the lasso rose gracefully in air and the noose fell over the steer's head. Immediately Baldy wheeled and started in the opposite direction. But the wary old steer was not to be caught napping and he wheeled before the rope had tightened and made after Baldy, head down like an avenging fury. Big Bill gave his horse the quirt and went after the steer, trying to get a second rope on him. But they were too fast for him. Although Baldy ran at his best pace, yet the steer gained steadily on him. Hank Brodie, looking over his shoulder, saw him bearing down on his horse like destruction incarnate.

With a sharp pull of his left hand on the reins, he

wheeled Baldy to the left while his right hand went to the holster for the .45. As the steer passed the revolver cracked. But, even so, the head-long flight of the deranged steer was not stopped. Again he turned and charged straight at the cow-puncher. Two more shots were fired and the steer fell head-long on the ground, almost between Baldy's knees.

"It was a close call," said Big Bill, riding up, "he mighty near ripped Baldy's flank open that time he went by. Lucky you had the gun along."

"It is never safe to ride a rod on the ranch without it. You see now," he continued to Larry, who had just ridden up, "that a .45 is sometimes indispensable."

"That is so," said Larry. "It is a lesson I never will forget. I had thought it was just nonsense, all you cow-punchers toting guns, but I see now it is necessary for the day's work."

"What made that steer act so like a demon?" inquired Larry as they jogged homeward. "I have never seen one behave like that before."

"Well," returned his uncle, "I should say for a guess without having looked him over that he was locoed, but Bill will examine him before they bury him and make a report to me.

"The loco weed is a serious menace to stock here on the western ranches. Of course, cattle do not make a business of eating it but they do get hold of it occasionally. There are two varieties, the Purple and the White, but the Purple is the most dangerous.

"The loco weed is to horses and cattle what opium and hashish are to men. First it intoxicates and enthralls them, but finally it masters them and takes away their reason. Your locoed horse or cow is a very dangerous animal and we shoot them on sight and count the cost later."

"Is a herd of cattle really dangerous?" asked Larry, after another pause. "They seem placid enough."

"Yes and no," returned his uncle. "A herd of cattle is treacherous like the sea. The sea will smooth out its billows with silver wavelets until it seems to be the most placid and harmless thing in all creation, but let a big wind strike it and soon it will kick up big billows that will smash the largest ship that floats and even beat down cliffs that have been eons in building. And so it is with herds of cattle. When they are feeding they are the most harmless looking creatures in the world. They are never hurried and occasionally stop to look about in a friendly manner. As long as man is on horse-back he is all right among them. I sometimes think they consider him a part of the horse, but let them discover him anywhere on the open plain afoot and it is quite another matter. First they will look at him inquiringly, then walk toward him slowly, soon the walk becomes a trot, and that in turn a mad gallop, until it would seem each is trying to outdo the other and be the first to the victim. If the unfortunate pedestrian cannot reach a friendly tree or some other shelter, he is good as dead and the chances are that when the herd has passed there won't be enough of him left for a respectable funeral. I have seen three men, first and last, who have been killed in this way and I never want to see another. It is a gruesome sight. Always remember, Larry, that you are perfectly safe in the presence of a herd as long as you are on horse-back, but never let them discover you afoot if you value your life."

CHAPTER IV

LARRY AND PATCHES

"WELL, Larry," said his Uncle Henry, the morning after the completion of the spring round-up, "I guess you and I had better get busy and break your colt. I think it is going to be a lively proposition and the sooner we get after him, the better."

"Break my colt!" repeated Larry in surprise. "Why, I haven't any colt. I don't own anything but the clothes I have on and a few in my old trunk."

"That is where you have another guess coming," returned his uncle, patting him affectionately on the arm. "You see I interviewed Mr. Morgan a week or so ago and bought the bay colt, the one you admired so much, from him and I am going to make you a present of him. He ought to make a fine saddle horse and a good cow-pony as well, and possibly a great running horse for he has the blood of some of the best Kentucky stock in his veins."

Larry was so overcome by this news that for several seconds he could not speak. A great lump filled his

68

throat and his eyes were full of tears. It was so unexpected and he had so admired the bay colt.

"How can I ever thank you, Uncle Henry?" he finally stammered. "You are so good to me."

"Tut, tut, boy," returned his uncle, "what is the use of having an old uncle if he cannot do you a good turn now and then?"

So, a few minutes later, armed with a hackamore, a fifty foot rope, and a lariat, Hank Brodie and his nephew made their way to the corral.

"You climb up on top of the corral fence," said Uncle Henry as he opened the gate cautiously. "It isn't any place for you inside. That colt has never had a rope touch him since he was two months old and I guess there will be fireworks."

So Larry climbed to the top of the corral fence and from that vantage point beheld the first lesson in breaking a wild colt.

The bay gelding although he was half mustang did not show this fact. The wild horses are usually ewe-necked and have light manes and tails, but this wild horse had a beautiful crest, and a heavy mane and tail. He was a bright bay with black points and black mane and tail and his weight was just a little under eleven hundred pounds. He had retained more of the characteristics of the Kentucky thoroughbred than of the wild horse. As he pranced about the corral, alert and snorting, Larry thought he was the most beautiful piece of horse flesh he had ever seen.

The bay colt had seen the men enter the corral and lasso other horses many times before, but hitherto they had never thrown a lasso at him, and somehow he had the notion he was immune. Hank Brodie waited until he was wedged against the fence between two other horses, then with a quick motion threw the lasso and the rope sailed gracefully through the air and caught the bay colt by both front legs. He gave two frenzied jumps and then threw himself heavily upon his right side. There he lay, struggling, kicking and squealing. Finally when he had quieted down a bit Hank approached him slowly, talking to him all the time. "Whoa, whoa, old boy, lie still. I won't hurt you," he said. Then he came close and put his hand, first on the horse's shoulder, then on his neck, and finally on his head, talking to him all the time. Then he put a hackamore upon the prostrate horse and took off the lariat.

The hackamore is a very strong halter usually made of horse hair. Sometimes a bit is worked into it and it also sometimes has a slip noose, then it is called a war-bridle. But this hackamore was just a plain halter. Then the broncho buster fastened the other end of the fifty foot rope to the snubbing post and let the colt pull until he had pulled himself to a standstill.

When the last vestige of pulling spirit seemed gone out of him for that day, the cow-puncher approached him with a saddle, but as this foreign object touched his back the bay colt snorted, reared and plunged. It was fifteen minutes before Uncle Henry could tighten even one cinch but patience will have its own reward and patience the horse-trainer must have. So in another fifteen minutes he had tightened the second cinch and replaced the hackamore with a bridle.

"He is going great, Larry," said his uncle, "I never had one behave as well before but I am sure there will be fireworks when I try to mount him."

When the cow-puncher tried to put his foot in the stirrup, the gelding kept pulling way from him but he finally got the horse up against the fence and managed to mount. As the man's weight settled in the saddle upon his back the bay colt bucked straight into the air at least a yard and then came down with his legs as stiff as fence posts. Larry was surprised at this behavior of the colt but he need not have been. For untold ages wild horses have bucked like this to dislodge mountain lions and other enemies which sought to pull them down. There was something in the consciousness of this wild horse that made him buck as his ancestors had always done. The next time he bucked he threw all four feet to the right while still in mid-air and it seemed to Larry that his uncle must be pitched from the saddle, but he kept his seat. Again the frantic colt tried the same maneuver but this time he threw his legs to the left. This strategy is called sunfishing, but the cow-puncher kept his seat and grinned pleasantly up at his nephew. Then he bucked and turned half way around as he came down so that when he struck his head was pointing where his tail had been. This was called swapping ends. But even this maneuver did not disturb the skillful broncho buster, but the colt's next move was more serious, for without any warning he reared straight in the air standing upon his hind legs. Even this maneuver had not been unexpected by the cow-puncher and as the frantic horse paused for a moment upon his hind legs the man slipped his left leg over the saddle and dropped to the ground, and not an instant too soon for almost at the same moment the horse toppled backwards and fell upon the ground, smashing the saddle tree as he fell. It was a close call and the cow-puncher had been lucky not to get a broken back or at least a broken leg, but he didn't seem to be disturbed by this catastrophe for he immediately sprang on the prostrate horse's head. The gelding squealed and kicked but all to no purpose, so he lay still.

"Now, Larry," said his uncle, "you go into the ranch house and get that cow-puncher book on the table.

There's a chapter in it I have been trying to get a chance to read and this is a good time."

A few minutes later when Larry returned with the book he found his uncle seated comfortably upon the horse's shoulder.

"You see," explained the cow-puncher as he lit a cigarette and prepared to read, "a horse cannot rise as long as you keep his head down and I am going to let him lie a spell and think it over."

So Larry climbed back to his perch on the corral fence while Hank Brodie smoked his cigarette and read his chapter in the book. At the end of half an hour he rose from his seat on the horse's shoulder and allowed him to get to his feet. The horse was trembling in every limb and was so cramped from lying on the ground that he could scarcely stand. The fight seemed all gone out of him for that day. He made no objection when the cow-puncher mounted him and jogged leisurely around the corral for fifteen minutes. Then Hank removed the saddle and bridle and set him free.

"Is he broken?" asked Larry, climbing down from his perch on the corral fence.

"Hardly," returned his uncle, "but this is the first lesson and I guess it was a good one. I don't think he will back-heave again. That is what we call that maneuver when he went over backwards. He had a good chance to think it over and I guess he has discovered it doesn't pay."

"How strange those four cream colored patches on either side of him make him look," said Larry. "It looks almost as though they had been put on with a paint brush."

"I guess his mother thought she would mark him after a paint at first and then changed her mind."

"What is a paint?" inquired Larry.

"A paint is cowboy slang for pinto and pinto is the Mexican name for painted, so there you have it."

"Those patches on his side have suggested just the name for him," cried Larry, excitedly. "I am going to call him Patches."

"It is a good name," returned his uncle, "it describes him to a T. It is always well to have the name for a horse mean something."

So from that very day the bay gelding became Patches and it was a name which afterwards won for his owner many distinctions.

The following morning Larry and his uncle were once more out in the corral giving Patches another lesson. To Larry's surprise they had to go over all the old ground again but even he noticed that the bucking was less pronounced. In two more lessons under the skillful handling of Hank Brodie, Patches had become quite docile and Larry asked if he might ride him.

HE'LL BE ONE OF THE GREATEST RUNNING HOSSES IN WYOMING

"Not just yet, son," replied his uncle. "It is all right for me to mount him but if you so much as tried to put your foot in the stirrup he would immediately buck you into kingdom come if he could.

"It is a very strange thing, but these wild horses can spot a tenderfoot and they are always waiting to give him a spill. But after a couple of weeks you can take a turn at him, even then it will be all you can do to keep from getting spilled."

About two weeks later, one evening, word was passed around among the cowboys that the kid was going to ride Patches to a finish. He was going to set him out. So most of the cowboys gathered around the corral to see the fun. They were seated upon nail kegs and boxes, cracking jokes at Larry's expense.

When Patches was at last brought out all bridled and saddled he looked docile enough and Larry did not think he would give him any trouble, but as soon as he was well in the saddle Patches bucked even more violently than he had with his uncle the first day. Straight into the air he bucked at least three feet and when he came down stiff-legged Larry thought that every tooth in his head hit against its fellow and every vertebra in his backbone received a terrible bang. Then without waiting to say as much as by your leave he sprang into the air sunfishing and his feet were thrown so violently to the right that Larry had to clutch the saddle horn to keep his seat.

"Pulling the lever," cried one of the cowboys. "Choking the horn," exclaimed another. "Chopping biscuit," cried a third.

"Aw, let the kid alone," growled Big Bill, "you don't want to see him killed, do you? He is doing all right."

Patches' next maneuver was to crowhop, after which he pulled off three or more running bucks. And each time his feet struck the ground it seemed to Larry that the breath of life would be jarred out of him but still he clung to the saddle. Then to the surprise of all the cow-punchers, Patches bolted. Straight through the ranch house yard he went and with a great leap cleared a high fence next to the wagon trail and disappeared down the road at a pounding gallop.

"Good Heavens," cried Pony running for the corral, "he'll kill the kid. I am going after him."

"I guess he will be all right," said Hank Brodie. "That boy is a pretty good horseman for his years and he will pull him down after a mile or two and he will come back looking like a different horse."

But Pony's fears could not be allayed and a moment later he galloped out of the yard on the Jack Rabbit and disappeared down the road.

Five minutes later the cow-punchers heard the sounds of returning hoofs. Larry and Patches were the first to come in sight and Pony and the Jack Rabbit were trailing a hundred feet behind.

Patches was still going at a good swinging gallop but not so fast as he had when he disappeared.

Larry guided him skillfully through the gate and by the ranch house.

"Head him into the corral fence," shouted his uncle as he passed. Larry did as he was commanded, and seeing his way blocked, Patches slowed down at the fence. Then Larry turned him about and rode him back to the ranch house. He was still snorting, prancing, and pulling on the bit, but well in hand.

"You done well, kid," cried Long Tom.

"You set him out," called Big Bill.

"We all knowed you could do it," cried Texas Joe, "he's your'n from now on."

This prophecy proved true, for although they had some lively tussles, Larry was always master after that.

"Uncle Henry," said the boy, the morning following his tussle with Patches, "I am going to train Patches in a different way from that you cowboys use. Now I have got the upper hand of him I am going to make him love me and make him do things for me because he wants to."

"That will be all right for you," returned Uncle Henry, "but it will take time. We cow-punchers cannot spend the time to fuss with them in that way."

Just about this time the cow-punchers turned their attention to the home ranch and Larry was given some of the range riding to do. At first he did this on Old Dobbin but after a week or two his uncle said he could take Patches and the boy's cup of joy was full.

It was irksome work for the cow-punchers riding on wheel harrows and sulky plows up and down the endless acres on the home ranch, but it was work that had to be done. They sweated and cussed but still they kept right at work and by the first of May, one hundred acres had been plowed and seeded.

In the meanwhile Larry had been busy training Patches and as he had promised his uncle he had moulded him through love and good-will.

After teaching him to turn to the right and the left in answer to the pressure of his knees on the sides, he taught him to stand when the lines were thrown over his head and left dangling on the ground. He also taught him the five paces of a saddle horse: the walk; the running trot which comes so natural to a mustang and is so easy on both horse and rider; then he developed the canter; and after that the gallop; and finally he taught him the Spanish walk.

The cow-punchers made many jokes at his expense. Big Bill said that he would have the horse's legs so tangled up that he wouldn't know whether he was coming or going. But Larry took their jokes good-naturedly and kept right on with his work.

Then he practised mounting while the horse was in motion, first at a walk, then a trot, and finally at a slow gallop. It took him nearly a week to master the gallop, but at last he got so he could mount when Patches galloped slowly by.

"What is all this here hoss play leading to anyhow?" inquired Big Bill one night. "Jest an ordinary hoss is good enough for me."

"Oh, I don't know," replied Larry, "you never can tell when some of these accomplishments will come in handy. I want Patches to be the best all-round saddle horse in these parts and a good cow pony as well."

"That is another story," said Hank Brodie, "it takes time to make a cow horse. A cow horse has got to know a lot, he has got to have horse sense. He has got to know a lot besides the cattle game; he must be able to ford rivers and keep out of quicksand, and if need be, to swim; he must keep his feet out of gopher and badger holes; he must know how to cut out cattle and how to head them back when he has got them out. He must be able to stand the strain of a lariat on a thousand pound steer when the steer is running at a gallop and he must also have sense enough to hold a lariat taut when a steer is thrown while the cow-puncher hog-ties him."

"Is there anything more?" inquired Larry in surprise. "That sounds like a liberal education."

"Oh, yes," returned his uncle, "there's all sorts of things and all sorts of difficulties coming up every day and your cow-pony must meet them with horse sense, some of it comes to him naturally but lots of it he has to learn."

After the hay on the home ranch had been cut and stacked there was a little lull in the ranch work and then it was that the cow-punchers, under the supervision of Larry, marked out a polo ground in the meadows close to the ranch house. Here on warm summer evenings they played many an exciting polo game.

Larry soon discovered, as Long Tom had intimated, that Big Bill's middle name was polo. For, mounted upon his big mustang, Manito, he was indeed a tower of strength and a defense of position. Long Tom himself upon the Panther was also good secondary defense while Larry and Pony played the forward positions. Larry himself had played many important polo games in the East. It was his ability to play polo that had made him a favorite with his riding master. He had several times been referred to in a local newspaper as the boy wonder. So under his guidance the C. C. Polo Team soon had an enviable reputation in the vicinity, defeating several good teams from neighboring ranches.

At first Patches did not take to the game as Larry had hoped. While he would gallop hither and yon at the touch of whip or spur, yet he did not seem to understand what it was all about. But one evening when he had been playing about two weeks it seemed to come to him in a flash. He got his eye on the ball and connected up with the idea that this was what they were after. From that time onward at the crack of the mallet he was after the ball like a cat after a mouse and he seemed to take as much interest in the game as any seasoned polo pony.

One evening when the cow-punchers had thought it too hot to play polo and the little company were lying on the grass by the ranch house, Hank Brodie made an observation that started a lively discussion.

"I have been thinking, boys," he said, "that Patches has got the makings of a great running horse and I wouldn't be at all surprised if he could trim the Jack Rabbit in a half mile dash any time." This statement from the head cow-puncher brought Pony to his feet with an excited explanation for if there was one thing in the world that he was proud of, it was the Jack Rabbit's ability to run in short races.

"He can't do it, Mr. Brodie," Pony cried excitedly, "there ain't a hoss in these here parts that can trim the Jack Rabbit in a half mile dash."

"Well," returned Mr. Brodie, "I don't see any way to settle it but to saddle them up."

This suggestion was as a match to gunpowder and Pony started for the corral on a run.

"Bill, you and Long Tom had better go along and make up a company. A race between two horses isn't very exciting."

So Larry and the other two cow-punchers went to the corral and five minutes later all returned, saddled and bridled.

"You take them down the road half a mile, Bill," said Hank Brodie, "and start by that big boulder in the bend of the road. You can start them with your gun. Joe and I will stay here at the scratch and watch the finish. We will be the judges."

All the cow-punchers were lined up beside the wagon trail, eager to see the race for hitherto the Jack Rabbit had always been successful in short races.

Almost before they knew it the crack of Bill's .45 rang out on the evening air and the race was on.

"How did they start, Joe?" asked Mr. Brodie after about ten seconds. Joe was watching through the field glass.

"The Rabbit got off like a rocket and he is now leading by four lengths and the rest of them are strung out, Patches bringing up the rear."

Joe reported again at the quarter, "They are coming jest about the same, perhaps the others have pulled up a little on the Jack Rabbit, but Patches is still behind."

At three-eighths the relative positions of the horses had not changed but the Jack Rabbit was now leading by only two lengths.

When they were about a hundred yards away Hank Brodie made a funnel of his hands and shouted to Larry and his voice rang out like the crack of a rifle.

"Give him the quirt, boy, give him the quirt."

Larry let the quirt fall, once, twice, and Patches

jumped forward in answer to this urge. At the same time there was born in his consciousness a new idea. It was not all his though, but was a part of his inheritance; an idea which came down through his blood from his Arabian ancestors, and from his great-grandfather who had broken the world's record at Churchill Downs. This was a race he was in; his master wanted him to beat the other horses; so immediately he lengthened his stride and quickened the beat of his hoofs.

In a hundred feet he had passed Bill, in a hundred feet more he had passed Long Tom and in the last hundred feet he shot past the Jack Rabbit like a whirlwind and finished a whole length ahead.

"Great jumping horn spoon!" cried Pony, pulling up fifty feet beyond the scratch. "That hoss didn't beat the Jack Rabbit, did he?"

"That's what he did," replied Hank Brodie. "Beat him by a length."

"There's some mistake about it," protested Pony. "Me and the Jack Rabbit didn't get a good start."

"Yes, you did," returned Hank. "We were watching you through the glass and you led by four lengths up to the quarter."

"Well, he couldn't do it again," said Pony. "Let's try again."

"No, I guess that is enough for to-night," returned Hank Brodie, "but if you tried it again and Larry gave him the quirt at the start, he would beat you by four lengths. Now I am going to make a prophecy about that horse. It is my opinion that before many years he will be one of the greatest running horses in Wyoming."

And the prophecy was a good one.

CHAPTER V

THE LONG, LONG TRAIL

EARLY in September the autumn round-up on the Crooked Creek Ranch was set in motion. Once more the parada of the ranch was marshalled on the lower plateau and the cattle were fed, a thousand at a time, into Piñon Valley. Here the spring and summer calves were branded while the beef cattle were cut out and driven to the home ranch. The beef cattle comprised the four year old steers and the barren cows. It was found when the round-up was finished that there were about a thousand beef cattle. This herd was turned into the cultivated lots on the home ranch where the rowen was knee high. They fell upon it with great zest and under these conditions put on flesh rapidly. They ate and ate of the green grass until they could eat no more and then rested only to eat again. So by the middle of November the cattle were in fine condition and ready for market.

Then it was that Hank Brodie made preparations for the drive to Wyanne. Saddles, bridles, and ponies were inspected and ten of the best cow-punchers selected for the trip.

86

When such old timers as Big Bill, Long Tom, and Pony saw these preparations going forward they became very mellow and reminiscent. Once again they recalled the days of long drives on the Santa Fé trail and of the handling of large herds of cattle on the Panhandle.

"Gosh almighty," said Big Bill, "this here country is getting too darn sophisticated for me. This here one day stand riding is too easy. It is too much like a woman's party with pink tea and drop the handkerchief. It ain't strenuous enough for your Uncle Bill. Why, in the old days there were Apaches on your trail, and rustlers rustling every thing you had, and the herd stampeding, and the devil to pay. Gosh, them was the days."

So, on a crisp autumn morning in the middle of November the herd of beef cattle were marshalled on the polo grounds. Two cow-punchers went at the head of the procession, not immediately in front of the cattle but on the sides. They were to steer the head of this great dragon as it crawled along the trail to Wyanne. One hundred yards further down the cavalcade were two more cow-punchers, and still another hundred further on another pair, with two others bringing up the rear. A large express wagon filled with camp blankets, a camp stove, and provisions followed behind.

For the first two days the trail led over adjacent

ranches and here they had to be careful that other cattle were not drawn into their own herd. Barways also had to be taken down and then put back again. Each day toward sundown a large open field had to be discovered and the cattle turned into it for the night. Here the cow-punchers rode round and round the herd until they had them moving around in a great circle. Little by little this motion lessened until finally the herd was at rest and they were ready for the night. Then the express wagon came up, the tents were pitched, the camp fire was built, and the cow-punchers prepared to eat a hearty evening meal. Whatever they had eaten thus far during the day since breakfast had been taken in the saddle.

It must not be supposed, however, that the herd was left unguarded during the night, for four cow-punchers were on guard, each with a shift of four hours. They rode round and round the herd continually and as they went they sang the cattle songs of the cowboys, those picturesque folk songs which have come down to us from the ranges of by-gone days.

Soon most of the cattle would be lying down, or standing and chewing their cuds, some would mill about for an hour or two but finally the entire herd would settle down for the night's rest. As soon as the herd had quieted down for the night the camp fire was kindled and one of the cow-punchers detailed to get

THEIR APPETITES NEVER APPEARED TO BE AS GOOD AS WHEN THEY
ATE IN THE OPEN

supper. Soon the aroma of frying eggs and bacon filled
the air and presently the cow-punchers were eating in
relays. And it seemed that their appetites were never
quite so good as when they ate out in the open.

After supper those not on guard of the herd would
gather around the fire and then it was that they grew
mellow and would spin many yarns of the old days, of
the cattle trails of long ago.

"Did I ever tell you gents about me and Little Al?"
inquired Big Bill, the first night as the cow-punchers
stretched out around the camp fire.

"Can't say as you hev, Bill," said Long Tom, winking at Larry and poking Pony Perkins in the ribs. They had all heard this story many times but whenever Bill offered to tell it, with accommodating memories they did not seem to remember.

"Well," said Bill, lighting a fresh cigarette, "It was this here way. I never knew where Little Al came from, he jest popped up one morning in camp. His real name was Alsandra Gonzales but I allus called him Little Al and he called me Uncle Bill. It was strange how we took to each other, seems as though I had knowed him allus when I had only seen him for a day or two.

"He was probably about twelve years old but he wan't bigger'n a pint of cider. He usen to ride on the pommel of my saddle in front of me and after a spell I got lonesome if he wan't a-perching there.

"But this here time I'm telling you about was after we'd knowed each other about a month. We had gone up into New Mexico to drive a part of our herd down onto the Panhandle. It was mighty dry that summer and water was scurse'n than hens' teeth. This night I'm telling you about, it seemed as though the entire Panhandle was as dry as a desert. The cattle hadn't had much of any water for two days and they was as restless as fleas and as uneasy as bees jest before swarming time. Finally on this here night we got them calmed down and ready for the night. We was located in a broad valley but jest below us it narrowed up sudden.

"It had been sort of sultry all day and I didn't like the looks of things. Me and Little Al was on guard with five others. We had six thousand cattle in the bunch. Pretty soon I began to notice lightning way off in the sky to the north but there wan't much thunder. I thought it was gonna go round us when all of a sudden the sky seemed to split wide open and there came a thunder clap like the crack of doom. Well, that was enough for the cattle. They was all on edge anyhow and every blasted one of them leaped to their feet. Some of them began bellowing and then the whole bunch stampeded. Almost before I knowed it, me and Little Al was surrounded on three sides with madly rushing cattle. Al seemed to sense our danger before I did.

" 'Senor,' he said, 'there isn't but one thing you can do, shoot old Mule-ears and then lie down behind him.'

"Al, says I, me and Mule-ears has been jogging along for quite a spell together and I ain't going to desert him now. Then I thought I felt something a-fumbling at my holster and the next thing I knowed my .45 cracked twice jest in front of my left knee. Little Al had reached over and got my gun and plugged old Mule-ears through the heart. He took two or three faltering jumps and then fell. I guess I must have been

stunned for the next thing I remembered I was lying
up close to something and something else was on top
of me. I opened my eyes and looked around. There
wan't a steer in sight. I was lying on the ground close
up to my hoss and Little Al was lying on top of me.
Half of his ribs was broken and he was terribly bat-
tered. He had layed above my head and sheltered me.
I was so stiff and bruised myself I could hardly get up
but Little Al was dead.

"He was the only greaser that I ever saw that I didn't
hate worse'n than the devil hates holy water but I really
did love Little Al."

It was a dramatic story as Bill told it and as Larry
gazed at the sun-burned, wind-tanned cowboy, he mar-
velled at his stoicism and the hardships he had seen.
But at this point in the reminiscences a cow-puncher
rode up saying it was time for a new shift. So Larry's
three friends, Big Bill, Pony, and Long Tom, saddled
their horses and went to keep guard. Above the sounds
of the milling herd a few minutes later Larry heard
Pony's clear tenor voice singing as he rode up and
down his beat and he was singing that old cow-puncher
hymn which Larry had heard that first night in the
Crooked Creek ranch house:

ROUNDED UP IN GLORY*

1. I've been thinking today, as my thought began to stray,
    Of your memory to me worth more than gold.
    As I ride across the plain, mid the sunshine and the rain
    You'll be rounded up in glory bye and bye.

Chorus

You'll be rounded up in glory bye and bye,
You'll be rounded up in glory bye and bye,
When the milling time is o'er,
And you'll stampede no more,
When He rounds you up, within the Master's fold.

2. May we lift our voices high, to that sweet bye and bye,
    And be known by the brand of the Lord;
    For His property we are, and He'll know us from afar,
    When He rounds us up in glory, bye and bye.

Chorus

You'll be rounded up in glory bye and bye,
You'll be rounded up in glory bye and bye,
When the milling time is o'er,
And you'll stampede no more,
When He rounds you up, within the Master's fold.

* *From Cowboy Songs collected by John A. Lomax, Macmillan Company.*

Fainter and fainter the song grew as Pony rode off in the distance. But in another five minutes from the other side of the herd Larry heard the click of a horse's shoes as he interfered and the soft jangling of the chains on the horse's reins. Then the mellow bass voice of Big Bill was lifted up in another cow-puncher ditty:

A HOME ON THE RANGE*

1. Oh, give me a home where the buffalo roam,
   Where the deer and and the antelope play,
Where seldom is heard a discouraging word,
   And the skies are not cloudy all day.

Chorus

Home, home on the range,
Where the deer and the antelope play,
Where seldom is heard a discouraging word,
And the skies are not cloudy all day.

2. Where the air is so pure, the zephyrs so free,
   The breezes so balmy and light,
For I would not exchange my home on the range
   For all of the cities so bright.

Chorus

Home, home on the range,
Where the deer and the antelope play,
Where seldom is heard a discouraging word,
And the skies are not cloudy all day.

* *From Cowboy Songs collected by John A. Lomax, Macmillan Company.*

A few minutes later Larry rolled himself up in his blankets on a bed of pine boughs by the camp fire. It had been a hard day, and notwithstanding a chilly wind and the distant howling of the coyotes he was soon sleeping soundly.

It did not seem to Larry that he had been sleeping five minutes when he was aroused by his uncle shaking him by the shoulder.

"Come on, son," he said, "it is our watch."

So Larry crawled reluctantly out of his warm blankets and he and his uncle and one other cow-puncher went to saddle their horses, and a few minutes later they relieved the other watch.

"You see," explained Uncle Henry, "we ride up and down around the herd, forty or fifty feet away from the cattle, just close enough to watch them and at the same time not to disturb them. You can sing if you want to, that will help to keep up your spirits. About this time of night the cattle are usually pretty quiet but two or three hours later they will get restless and begin to mill about. The two hours before daylight are the most dangerous period of the entire night watch, but everything is going to be all right tonight."

So Larry and Patches began their night vigil going up and down, while Larry sang to the cattle. He did not know many of the cattle songs so his repertoire was soon exhausted but he filled in with such old favorites

as Seeing Nellie Home, Just Before The Battle, and
Swanee River. It was very dark as the moon had set
and the sky was overcast, but Patches seemed to know
what was expected of him and he walked steadily up
and down the quiet beat. Every ten minutes Larry
would meet his uncle at the end of his beat. Then they
would exchange salutations and turn their horses about
and go over the beat again.

It seemed to Larry that the hours were endless.
Would his watch never cease? But after what seemed
to him to be the whole night the first gray shimmer of
light appeared in the East. Even before this warning
of the coming day some of the cattle had been up and
stirring about. Several times he had had to drive these
restless ones back into the herd for the orders were to
keep them closely bunched until daylight.

Finally the gray streak in the East warmed into the
crimson telling of the birth of a new day, then the rosy
tints grew brighter and brighter and finally Old Sol
peeked up over the rim of the eastern hills and the new
day had really come; Larry and Patches were certainly
glad to see it.

Soon they were back at the camp fire which was
now burning brightly for one of the cow-punchers was
getting breakfast. It seemed to Larry that fried saus-
ages and hard-tack dipped in hot coffee tasted better
than any beefsteak breakfast he had ever eaten in

his whole life. The cowboys ate in relays, so by eight o'clock the cavalcade once more formed and the long day's march began.

By noon the old cattle trail which they had been following emerged into the travelled highway, or wagon trail as they called it, and they were out on the open prairies, in the land of the purple sage, where the land had been homesteaded and broken up into sections, quarter-sections, and half-sections. Here the wagon trail was sixty-six feet wide with a fence on either side. This helped the cow-punchers for the task of keeping the cattle bunched was now greatly lessened, but it also added to their difficulties for often they encountered horseback riders, buckboards, and lumber wagons and all of these greatly impeded the movement of the herd. But they kept patiently plodding along and by twilight had covered fifteen miles.

They found just the right spot, a quarter-section of sage brush, a lot which no homesteader had cared to preëmpt. So here the herd was brought to rest and once again the camp fire burned brightly. The cow-punchers ate in relays and then went to the night watch.

By noon of the third day of the drive the weather had changed suddenly, the clear crisp air had been succeeded by a warm balmy breeze. It was as sudden as that in the springtime when Chinook breathes over the landscape and in a few hours drives winter back and announces that spring has come.

So now the autumn time was driven back and the temperature of summer prevailed. The landscape was diffused with a soft blue haze which told plainly that a wonderful spell of Indian summer had come.

Larry greeted this change of weather with delight. The mornings had been so frosty and the nights so cold and chilly that it was a relief to turn back to summer conditions. But when he remarked upon this fact to his brother cow-punchers as they jogged along beside the herd he got only a disgruntled answer.

That evening as they ate by the cheerful camp fire it seemed to Larry that a sudden depression had come over the cow-punchers, even such jovial spirits as Big Bill and Pony Perkins seemed subdued. It was inexplicable to Larry, so he finally asked them what was the matter.

"What's got into you boys, Uncle Bill?" he said between two gulps of hot tea. "You all act as dumb as oysters. Anybody would think this was a funeral procession instead of a jolly cattle drive."

"Wal," returned Bill scanning the sky carefully in every direction, "I dunno, perhaps everything's all right. We won't cross any bridges until we come to them, but I don't like this darn hot weather. It ain't seasonable and when it tunes up in this way we're always sure to catch something."

"Why, I think it's just great," returned Larry. "We won't have to have any camp fire to sleep by tonight."

"Wal, perhaps you're right," returned Bill, "I hope so."

A few minutes later Larry's three friends went to take up their night watch while he rolled up in his blankets to sleep.

In what seemed an incredibly short time his uncle was shaking him by the shoulder telling him to get up as it was their watch.

"I don't like the feel of things," remarked Uncle Henry as they jogged around to their position. "Perhaps it's going to be all right but it is terribly sultry and I wish it was twenty degrees cooler."

It was much darker this night then it had been the nights previous so Larry gave Patches his head most of the way. About all he could do was to keep him close up to the herd and this he was able to do by the sound of the milling cattle.

As the hours wore on, it grew darker and darker and still more muggy, and though it was strangely still sound seemed to carry a long way. He could distinctly hear the sound of Old Baldy's hoofs fifty rods away as his uncle rode up and down the line.

It must have been about five o'clock, the danger

hour to a sleeping herd, when Larry noticed far off on the western horizon fitful flashes of lightning and then distant thunder. As the last peal died away he heard his uncle's .45 crack twice. This was the signal in the camp, should they happen to hear it, for all of the force to mount and stand ready for whatever might happen.

But the distant lightning became brighter and brighter and the thunder more pronounced and Larry could hear the cattle stirring uneasily. Then the same thing happened that he remembered having heard Big Bill describe the first night as they sat about the camp fire listening to his yarn of Little Al. For without an instant's warning the heavens seemed to crack wide open; for a hundred-thousandth part of a second it was as bright as day. He could see the great herd of cattle, some lying down and some standing. He could see distant trees and bushes, and then as suddenly as it had come this light went out and it was followed by a peal of thunder like the crack of doom.

As by a common impulse this brought the cattle to their feet in great alarm and here and there was heard a frenzied bellow. Then again there was that strange lurid light, a great crack in the heavens, and a peal of thunder that was fairly deafening. That was enough for the now nearly frenzied herd and with one accord the entire thousand cattle bolted, with heads down, tails up, and utter terror in the mind of each.

Larry's first impulse when he saw this terrible manifestation of the herd was to turn Patches in the opposite direction and ride as far away from this thundering monster as possible. But this was only for an instant, then the code and spirit of the cowboy asserted itself. He knew that the cow-puncher was a soldier and his post of duty was the night watch; his first duty was to his employer and his second consideration was for his own life and limbs. He remembered also that this herd of cattle was under the special guardianship of his uncle; his uncle was responsible for tens of thousands of dollars; this uncle who had done so much for him. He would not fail him now. So, as the herd, one thousand strong, racing madly they knew not where, rushed off in the darkness, Larry reined Patches in as close to the herd as he dared and galloped by the side of the frenzied cattle.

But as Patches raced through the darkness, picking his own way, a terrible fear seized Larry. Where were they going? What was ahead of them? What would the next jump bring forth? Was the way clear or would they plunge into some gorge or flounder in some morass? But in this dilemma he was entirely helpless and could merely give Patches his head and trust to the fine horse's splendid instinct to carry them safely through this terrible crisis.

Again Larry heard his uncle's revolver crack three

times and he knew this was the signal by which he wanted to locate the rest of the cow-punchers, so Larry answered with three quick shots.

But he had barely replaced the revolver in the holster when Patches seemed to pause for a moment in his flight and Larry felt the horse's muscles grow tense beneath him. Then without warning the horn of his saddle shot up and struck Larry a stinging blow in the breast and at the same time the back of Patches' neck hit him in the face. For a moment they seemed to hang in mid-air and then Patches came down to earth with a loud slap of his hind feet, and the strange maneuver was plain to Larry. They had jumped a high fence. How in the world, in total darkness and travelling at the time at a gallop, had the splendid horse seen this obstacle in time to save both of their lives?

But the cattle were not so fortunate. They did not possess the night eyes and instinct of Patches and they went crashing into the fence like an avalanche. Crash, smash, crash went the poles and Larry could hear the sound of breaking stakes and fence poles for a hundred yards down the line to his left. This sound was interspersed with the bellows of terrified cattle and the groans of those who had been injured. But there was no time to stop and see what it all meant for the herd leveled the fence as a cyclone would have done and swept on through the darkness. A minute or two

PATCHES GAVE A GREAT LEAP

later Patches stumbled and nearly pitched Larry out of the saddle, only his desperate clinging to the saddle horn saved him. It had been a badger hole that had nearly brought horse and rider to earth, but they just escaped and Patches galloped on. Minutes seemed like hours and with each rod that they covered the horror of this headlong flight through the inky night grew upon Larry.

Presently Patches paused again for a second in his mad gallop and the next thing Larry knew they were sliding down a steep embankment, the horse sliding on his haunches with his fore-legs thrust out in front of him. Larry could hear the sliding of sand and gravel and soon they were at the bottom of a gulch. In less time than it takes to tell they were scrambling up the farther side.

But here again the cattle did not fare as well as horse and rider and Larry heard them as they fell into the bottom of the gulch. One, two, a half dozen, and a dozen, but still the mad flight of the terrified herd swept on.

At this point Larry noticed that Patches was pulling off to the right and away from the herd, so he pulled him sharply to the left and once again galloped alongside. It seemed to him that the pace of the maddened cattle was slackening, or was it his frantic hope that tried to realize this cheering sign?

He had begun to think that possibly the worst of the flight was over when Patches plunged into a fringe of bushes and once again they began sliding down a steep bank. After forty or fifty feet had been covered Patches gave a great leap and the next instant water splashed up into Larry's face and the horse sank to his middle in a swift-moving current.

Larry's first thought was that they were lost, but Patches was equal to the situation for as soon as the water became deep he began swimming leisurely. Then came another illuminating flash from the heavens and Larry saw to his consternation that they were swimming in a great river. A score of cattle were swimming in the river near him while hundreds of others were huddled on the bank nearby. But a greater part of the herd had been turned by the river and most of the mad procession were sweeping upstream.

Another blinding flash a minute later revealed his uncle upon Old Baldy swimming in the river nearby.

"Thank God you're safe, boy," cried Uncle Henry. "I guess we've had the worst of it. This is the La Platte river and it has turned the stampede. I guess we will be able to stop them now. You make your way ashore as soon as you can but be very careful and don't get into quicksand. Give Patches his head."

So Larry turned Patches about and guided him to the shore. When they were about thirty feet from the bank, to his surprise Patches snorted and began backing water, and Larry headed him downstream. Here he again evinced fear, so Larry tried still another spot. Here Patches found good footing and soon they were on terra firma. Then Larry and the faithful horse climbed back through the bushes where he was soon joined by his uncle. Torrents of rain now began to fall and the lightning ceased, and as the cow-punchers said "they had weathered the storm" although it seemed to Larry that they were in the midst of the very worst of it.

Soon the cowboys kindled small camp fires around the frightened herd, then began co-ordinating and quieting down the cattle. Half an hour later daylight came and then they went to look for the stragglers.

Larry found the place where he and Patches had cleared a six-foot pole fence. Here they found half a dozen cattle; three of them with broken legs, one punctured by a stake, and two dead. At the gulch where he and Patches had passed over in safety a dozen more cattle had succumbed, while in the river they had lost nearly twenty, part of these had been drowned in the swift current and the rest caught in the quicksand which Patches had avoided through his wild horse sagacity.

Altogether they had lost thirty-five head of cattle but some of these were partly salvaged by shooting them and selling them to the local farmers for beef. It took the better part of that day to get the herd once more in travelling condition, but by the middle of the afternoon they were on the way again.

Three days later the little cavalcade trekked into Wyanne and the cattle were safely coralled in the shipping pens at the freight yards. Then Hank Brodie received a receipt for the entire herd with the exception of the thirty-five cattle which had been lost in the stampede. They were a tired though happy lot. They had seen hardship and danger, and they had met both like men, and for this time the long, long trail had come to an end.

CHAPTER VI

THE COW-PUNCHERS VS. THE GRAY HORSE TROOP

WITH the nine hundred sixty odd cattle of the Crooked Creek drive safe in the shipping pens at the freight yards at Wyanne, and with the receipt for the same in his pocket, a great load was lifted from the mind of Hank Brodie. His cow-punchers also shared in this relief and entered into the remainder of their visit in Wyanne with the exuberance of school boys. It had been a hard drive although not a very long one, but the stampede, considering the size of the herd, had been a serious one. Even such old timers as Big Bill, Long Tom, and Pony Perkins admitted that they had had enough for the present.

The cow-punchers spent the following day in resting up after their arduous labors with the drive, and looking about the town. In the afternoon they visited the military post and had a little practice on the soldiers' polo grounds.

For the secondary object of the cow-punchers' visit to Wyanne was the playing of a match polo game with the Gray Horse Troop. This event had been announced to the town and to all the surrounding coun-

109

try for fifty miles in every direction. This had been accomplished by means of some large and striking posters which had been displayed in shop windows and upon fences. These posters depicted the polo grounds with four cow-punchers upon their bronchos riding at a terrific pace down the field; while the Gray Horse Troop was backed up in front of their goal defending the honor of the regiment.

This troop of cavalry, as its name indicated, was composed entirely of gray horses which the Commissary Department had secured after a great deal of pains. This was the show troop of the regiment and it was always seen on state occasions. Not only that but among its men were some of the best polo players in the regiment as well as some fine polo ponies. The polo team of the Gray Horse Troop had been champion of the state for several years, but the fame of the Crooked Creek team had been wafted to them on the wings of the west wind and two weeks before Hank Brodie and his cow-punchers had started out on their drive, they had received a challenge from the Gray Horse Troop to play a match game of polo on their grounds at the military post two days before Thanksgiving. The challenge had been gladly accepted and now the cow-punchers turned all of their feverish energies towards the successful culmination of the contest.

For experienced horses and individual players the troopers had every advantage, for while the cow-punchers had only three changes of ponies, the troopers had four. But the cow-punchers were a carefully co-ordinated team. They did not care who got the goal so long as they won. None of them were stars with the possible exception of Larry, but all were terrific workers. They had been trained in a hard school. The cavalry men with all their maneuvers and long marches had never seen such grilling work as the cow-punchers had. Besides, their work among the cattle had helped them for the strenuousness of polo.

Big Bill mounted upon Manito played the defense position, Long Tom on the Panther the secondary defense, while Pony on the Jack Rabbit and Larry on Patches played the forward positions. For their second string of ponies they had Hank Brodie's horse, Baldy, and three pintos. While for their third string they had two bays and two grays. This meant that the horses that started the first chukker had to play three periods and two are considered the usual limit.

On the other hand the troopers had four shifts of horses. They usually started with their grays; the second chukker was played with their bays, the third with their brown ponies and the fourth with their blacks. The second half was played in the same order as the first.

The polo field was located on the troopers' training grounds. It was the usual size, three hundred yards long and one hundred and fifty wide. The goal posts were twenty-four feet apart and the center line bisected the field in the middle from right to left.

The morning of the eventful day dawned bright and clear. The spell of Indian summer which had endured for the past three or four days had given way to a brisk north wind. It was typical football weather and a great day for polo.

Wyanne was gay with colors and many visitors were in town for the match. Cow-punchers and cattle men had come from every part of the state while the troopers also had their champions. When the cow-puncher team went onto the field they were amazed at the crowd. Their own supporters were lined up on the left side of the field. There were cow-punchers galore on horseback dressed in the usual regalia. There were buckboards and spring wagons and large parties in lumber wagons. In order not to be outdone by the troopers the cow-punchers had hired a large brass band. On the opposite side of the field the supporters of the Gray Horse Troop were lined up. Nearly the entire regiment was there with their military band while the townspeople and many visitors from surrounding towns also supported the troopers. There were women on horseback with their escorts, in dog-carts, and in buckboards, and also many a smart carriage and carryall.   For this polo match was a great event in Wyoming.

As captain of the team, Big Bill gave his men their last instructions.

"Don't forget for a minute, gents," he said, "that we're jest as good as they be.   Our first string of hosses can't be beat in these parts and we'll only fight the game one chukker at a time.   Now, gents, this will be our policy, get their goats at the start, get hold of the ball and keep it hanging for about four minutes then we will cut loose and show them all what we can do.   This will take as little as possible out of our best string of hosses and we got to use our minds.   As far as hosses are concerned they have got us whipped before we start but we jest got to use our beans.   So go at them, boys, for the honor of the cow-punchers of Wyoming."

Then the military band played the Star Spangled Banner while the cow-puncher's band responded with Hail, Columbia, and Marching Through Georgia. Then the referee called the captains together for the start and the teams lined up for the throw-in.   Three players from each team lined up opposite each other about six feet apart each on their own side of the center line, while the defense man on each side played about twenty yards back towards his own goal.   Then the referee tossed the ball along the alley between the teams and the game was on.

Larry and the first trooper locked mallets and the ball rolled on to the second pair. Pony and the second trooper executed the same maneuver. Then Long Tom, whose arms were a tremendous length, reached out and with a skillful twist of his wrist shot the ball back under the horses of the cow-punchers. It only rolled a few yards but that was all that Long Tom wanted. Like a flash the three cow-punchers wheeled and before the troopers knew what their next play would be they had formed in a little closely-packed triangle about the ball.

The troopers rode 'round and 'round this triangle reaching for the ball from every possible position, but the bronchos merely shifted their positions enough to keep them away from the ball. As soon as it rolled out into danger one of the cow-punchers leaned over and tapped it back to the open spot between them.

The crowd, especially the supporters of the troopers, were entirely nonplussed by this maneuver. This was a form of strategy that the cow-punchers had been practising nearly every evening all through the summer. In the technique of polo this was called keeping the ball hanging, but in the phraseology of Big Bill it was just treading on the ball.

Presently the men from the regiment began shouting to their comrades. "Get that ball! Poke it out! Play polo! Start the game! What are you doing, treading water?" Meanwhile the supporters of the cow-punchers were filled with glee and shouted their derision across the polo field.

The troopers attacked the little triangle from every side. They tried to spur their ponies through between the cow-punchers' ponies, but this crowding and pushing game was a part of the day's work for the bronchos for during the round-up season they did little else. They were in the habit of crowding a steer that weighed three or four hundred pounds more than they did, so in this football polo they were right in their element.

"I say," growled the captain of the troopers' team, after a couple of minutes of futile efforts to break through and get the ball, "if you don't want to play the ball let us have it. You will ruin the game."

"Oh, hurry up," put in another trooper, "you fellows will want to get home and milk the cows."

"We ain't in no hurry," growled Long Tom, "our cows will wait as long as your hosses."

Whenever the ball was in danger from one side of the triangle some one would tap it across to the other. Once it bounded out into the open and was nearly lost. But by this time the supporters of the troopers had become nearly frantic. "Start to play," they yelled. "Get going."

Even the friends of the cowboys began to look serious. This was not the sort of game they had expected.

Then at a signal from Big Bill which indicated that four minutes of the chukker had already passed, Long Tom reached down and with a quick stroke shot the ball over to Bill who was watching for it and he in turn drove it sharply down the field in an oblique direction while the cow-puncher supporters yelled with delight. Their favorites had broken loose and the fun was on.

At the crack of Bill's mallet Larry was off to the right side of the field following the ball while Pony galloped for the left and Long Tom took up his position in the middle, half way between them, while the defense man for the troopers raced back towards his goal and the rest of the troopers tried to break up the triangular drive of the cow-punchers.

Larry overtook the ball just before it went out of bounds at the right side of the field and cracked it over to Long Tom who relayed it to Pony Perkins at the left side. It must not be imagined that the troopers had been idle all this time, for a gray horse rider was after each of the cowboys trying to upset his play. Pony's next drive sent the ball back to the middle of the field just in time to escape a galloping trooper and Long Tom relayed it to Larry not a second too soon.   The ball had now moved up to within fifty yards of the goal post and the troopers' defense man had come out to anticipate a possible shot, but Larry had no intention of trying for a goal.   Instead he relayed the ball back to Long Tom who was also about fifty yards from the goal post and in the middle of the field.   So the gray horse defense man moved over to meet this new threat and two of his teammates joined him, but Long Tom had no intention of shooting, for like a flash he shot the ball back to Larry and he in turn drove it between the goal posts only two feet inside the right hand post and the cow-punchers had drawn first blood.

Then the teams changed goals and lined up again for the throw-in.   This time the troopers secured the ball and started the drive towards the cow-punchers' goal, but before it was well under way the referee's whistle sounded for the end of the chukker and the two teams trotted off to the stables to change their mounts.

"Thank heaven that's over," said Big Bill.

"Me and the Jack Rabbit ain't wet a hair," said Pony.

"Patches didn't even get limbered up," put in Larry.

"The Panther didn't even know we were playing," said Long Tom.

"That was my strategy," said Big Bill. "Heaven only knows how much we will have to use these hosses before we get through this here game so I planned to rest them all I could. This next chukker will be different. It will have to be billiards from the start. Bang! Whiz! Zip! We got to do some fancy riding this chukker, gents, we got to protect our one-point lead."

In less time than it takes to tell, the saddles were put on fresh horses and the two teams started back to the grounds. This time Larry was mounted upon Baldy, and the other three cowboys on pintos, while the troopers were mounted on their bays.

Larry secured the ball at the throw-in and tapped it back beneath Baldy's feet. He whirled like a flash and Larry hit the ball again, driving it over to Big Bill who was watching for it. As the cowboys' defense man with his powerful right arm drove the ball far down the field into the troopers' territory Larry and Pony were after it riding like the wind.

But the troopers' rover was too quick for them for he intercepted the ball and drove it back and two of his team-mates followed his lead and soon the three were sweeping down the field in a sort of drag-net formation, each carrying the ball in turn and passing it quickly from one to another in short snappy passes. The cow-punchers checked back rapidly in front of the advance trying to get in and secure the ball but they could not stem the rush.   When the ball was within seventy-five yards of the cow-punchers' goal Larry got in ahead of the trooper who was after it and with a skillful left-side stroke drove it out of bounds.   Here the teams again lined up for the throw-in.   This time the cowboys secured the ball and started down the field in their triangular formation using long passes obliquely across the field.   In each pass they gained a few rods until they were within sixty yards of the troopers' goal when they again lost the ball and it started back down the field.

It was just the kind of polo the crowd enjoyed, full of hard riding, brilliant strokes, and great suspense. Back and forth the ball flew.   First one goal was threatened and then the tide would turn and the other team would be on the defense, backed up to their goal post.   It was hard to tell which had the better of it. All eight players were superb riders and their mounts were good and all of the ponies knew the game.

A little luck on either side, a missing of a stroke, and a lucky shot might have scored, but as it happened the chukker ended with the ball absolutely in the middle of the field where it had started and the two teams trotted off again for fresh mounts.

"Wal, gents," said Big Bill, "we got along all right so far, but this here chukker that's coming is going to be a tough one. These here ponies we're going to ride now ain't ever connected up fully with the idee that they are to follow the ball. Of course they are good hosses and will go where we rein them and will mind the whip and the spur, but they ain't got real polo intelligence. We'll simply do the best we can and let it go at that. Don't forget for a minute, gents, that we are jest as good riders as they be. Their business is living in the saddles and ourn is the same. Stick to them, boys, and make them fight for every inch they get."

This chukker the troopers had the advantage from the start for they secured the ball and immediately started for the cow-punchers' goal using their short quick passes and the drag-net offensive. In almost no time they were threatening the cow-punchers' goal. Big Bill with a stroke like the hammer of Thor lifted the ball which was skipping towards his goal high in air over the troopers' heads. To the great amazement of the spectators it fell squarely in the middle of the field. Soon the troopers were hammering away at their goal again and in three minutes and forty-five seconds after the beginning of play they scored while the regiment and their supporters went wild. The band played Stars and Stripes Forever in acknowledgment of Uncle Sam's troopers.

But nothing daunted by this turn of the fortunes of war the cow-punchers rode back to the middle of the field determined to stem the tide of war which had turned against them. They secured the ball on the throw-in but could only hold it for a few seconds as the troopers' ponies were superior to theirs. Soon it was flying towards their goal carried by this irresistible three-man offensive and the short quick passes. Within fifty yards of their own goal the cow-punchers secured the ball and kept it hanging for a couple of minutes and it almost seemed as though they would ward off another score when with a lucky stroke from one of the troopers the ball went through and the score was two to one in favor of the soldiers.

But this was the end of their scoring for this chukker as the referee's whistle sounded and the cowboys were glad to hear it.

"These here grays and bays are going to be the ruination of us," said Big Bill. "We are as good as they be on our best hosses but we ain't got a smell-in on these here mounts. I don't jest know what we are going to do, but we are going to keep on fighting."

The fourth chukker was a direct replica of the first. The cowboys secured the ball on the throw-in and immediately formed a small hollow traingle, keeping the ball hanging. The troopers milled 'round and 'round the little triangle trying to ride through between the closely bunched horses and poked with their mallets for the ball, but they did not get it. Their supporters yelled at them to poke it out, to play polo, while the supporters of the cow-punchers were jubilant. Once the troopers got the ball, when a horse accidentally hit it and knocked it out, and started a drive down the field, but they soon lost the ball and again the cowboys resorted to their football tactics. In this manner they kept the ball hanging for five minutes of the chukker and then they broke loose. Once again they began their triangular drive down the field, Larry on the right, Long Tom in the center and Pony at the left. The troopers galloped hither and yon trying to intercept the ball or to put the cow-punchers out of play, but if one of the men at the side was covered, Long Tom shot the ball back to the other and he immediately started dribbling down the side line. It was impossible for the troopers to cover all three men at once so they could not stop the irresistible drive of these knights of the lariat.

Finally they carried the ball down to the fifty-yard line. Each trooper tried to cover his man and prevent the play. Larry drove the ball across to Long Tom, and Pony rode in closely as though he expected to receive the ball. This drew the troopers over to that

THE COW-PUNCHERS SWEPT BY WITHOUT LOSING THE BALL

side of the goal and Long Tom immediately drove the ball back to Larry and he in turn shot it through between the posts on the unguarded side and the score was tied.

The cowboys' friends yelled with delight.   For a few minutes pandemonium reigned but the chukker was nearly over.   The referee's whistle sounded before play could be resumed.

"Wal, boys, we've tied them up so far," said Bill, "and we ain't very badly blowed yet but the wurst is yet to come."

There was a fifteen minute intermission between the halves and this gave the cow-punchers a chance to hold a council of war.   Bill called them together and they talked the situation over while they were waiting for their new ponies.

"We are all set for the next chukker," said Bill, "our hosses are all right, but what bothers me is the sixth chukker.   Our bays and grays nearly ruined us the last time we rode them."

"I've been thinking about that," said Pony, "but I don't see what else we can do.   We can't kill our best hosses."

"Why not play our first string for the sixth chukker and put the pintos and Baldy up for the seventh," said Long Tom.

"Baldy won't stand it," put in Hank Brodie who was

standing on the outskirts of the council, "he isn't as young as he used to be."

"Well," said Larry, "there is one thing we can do. Play our best string the sixth, the pintos for the seventh and substitute Patches for Baldy, and then play our best string in the eighth."

"Man alive," ejaculated Big Bill, "you don't want to kill that hoss of yours, do you?"

"I don't think it would kill him," returned Larry confidently. "I don't think you gents know Patches. He is made of iron, he is one horse in a thousand, there won't anything kill him."

"Sounds mighty good to me," said Bill. "If you want to risk Patches we'll put her through."

"Now remember, gents," warned Big Bill, just before they mounted for the fifth chukker, "our policy is to feed the kid. He can shoot to beat anybody on our team and there ain't any hoss in these here parts that can touch Patches. So we'll feed the kid. And don't forget, gents, what we've been through in the last two days. This here polo game is a lady's promenade compared with it. Fellows that have ridden hell-bent through darkness as black as a stack of black cats, going God only knows where, at the head of a thousand fear-crazed steers ain't a-going to show the white feather in any polo game. So jest buck up, boys, and do your darndest."

The fifth chukker was a lively one and the honors were equally divided. The troopers secured the ball on the throw-in and carried it irresistibly down the field. Long Tom and Big Bill both missed easy strokes and before the cowboys knew it a goal had been scored. But they came back strong and tied it up in the last two minutes of play. Once again they carried the ball down the field with their triangular defense until they had reached the fifty-yard line, but for some reason—which the troopers did not understand, Long Tom and Larry had changed positions and Larry was playing at the center. Again the troopers put up a stiff resistance. Long Tom drove the ball over to Larry. It was a ricochetting shot, skimming along the grass in easy bounds. Larry caught it six inches above the ground and with an easy stroke lobbed it over the heads of the amazed troopers and dropped it fairly between the goal posts. It was a beautiful play and wholly unexpected and the cowboy's band celebrated by playing the "Arkansas Traveler" and "The Girl I Left Behind Me," while all of the cow-punchers shouted themselves hoarse.

But nothing daunted the troopers rode on for the sixth chukker. This they expected would be easy for they knew the cow-punchers would have to use their poor string of ponies. But they were an astonished polo team when the cow-punchers trotted on the field mounted upon their best horses.

"Horse killers," yelled somebody in the regiment.

"What are you trying to do to those horses?" shouted another.

But the cow-punchers, all unmindful of this ridicule, took their places. The sixth chukker was nip and tuck. The ball flew up and down the field, but neither team could carry it successfully for any length of time. Sooner or later some one missed a stroke or was put out of play and the ball fell into the opponent's hands.

Again and again Larry and Pony rode down the field behind the trooper who was carrying the ball. Larry would ride in on his right flank just before he reached the ball and as he made the stroke would hook his mallet and Pony would pick up the ball and start it back down the field.

It was a chukker of hard riding, brilliant strokes and many close calls for the defense men. Once the troopers drove the ball over the cow-punchers' goal line, but it was six inches outside the post and the cowboys got a free shot from the back line and this carried the ball out of danger. So the chukker ended with the score still three to three.

The troopers were not surprised to see the cow-punchers come back with the pintos for the seventh, for they reasoned that the other ponies would be out of the question, but they were astonished to see Patches

still in the game.   Any other horse would have been
dripping with sweat and white with lather, but he
seemed as fresh as he had in the first chukker.   His
quick gallops up and down the field, and Larry's sure
stroke together with the fine defense work of the cow-
punchers' team again held the troopers scoreless and
the seventh chukker ended with the score tied.

The troopers rode on the field for the last chukker
full of confidence.   They felt sure that the cowboys
would now have to use one of the poor strings in
which case the soldiers looked for a walk-over, but
instead the cow-punchers came to the throw-in riding
their same old string.   All of the ponies but Patches
had already played three full chukkers and Patches
had been in the game for four and now was starting
the fifth.   It was unheard of, two chukkers were usually
considered the limit and this game had been fast and
furious, but the bay horse was still going strong and
looked like the best pony on the field.

Again the spectators were treated to brilliant polo.
First the troopers took the ball and carried it within
striking distance of the opponents' goal, but through
a bad shot lost the chance to score.   Then the cow-
punchers' team failed in the same manner.   Back and
forth the game swayed.   The suspense was terrific.
A lucky shot, or a miss of an easy stroke would turn
the scale.   There was no talking or jesting in the

crowd now. Absolute silence reigned. The attention of every one was riveted on the desperately riding players.

When the play had been going for about six minutes the troopers took the ball at the middle of the field and carried it down within striking distance of their opponents' goal, but they lost it through the brilliant playing of Pony and Larry, and the cow-punchers once again started an offensive. Little by little they worked the ball up the field until they were within one hundred yards of their opponents' goal. There was one minute to go, and realizing this fact Big Bill decided to forsake his position as defense man, and, putting spurs to Manito went down the field at a keen gallop after his team mates, determined to do or die.

The troopers were now checking back towards their own goal post. Could they stem the onward rush of the cow-punchers who were carrying the ball with short quick passes? As they neared the fifty-yard line Bill caught up with them and joined the mad rush towards the troopers' goal post. The soldiers were game as Uncle Sam's good fighters always are, but the cow-punchers swept by them, and through them without losing the ball. It was never quite plain to the spectators who shot it through at last for both Larry and Pony struck at the same time. Big Bill and Manito were also in the play and they went crashing into the troopers' right goal post just as Larry and Pony swept through on the other side.   The falling post hit Larry a terrific blow on the head as he passed.   His first impression was that one of the troopers had struck him with his mallet and then he remembered that they were good sportsmen and gentlemen, and would not do such a thing.   He had just sense enough left to hang to the horn of his saddle with one hand, and to clutch Patches' mane with the other.   The next thing he remembered he was lying on the grass and some one was throwing water in his face.   His Uncle Henry was bending over him.   He could hear a great shouting from the crowd but it sounded a long way off.   He didn't even know just where he was.   But presently his senses cleared and he plainly heard his uncle's voice calling to him.   "Larry, Larry, can you hear me?   Wake up, boy.   Are you coming round?" inquired Uncle Henry anxiously.

For answer Larry pressed his uncle's hand and said feebly, "Oh, yes, I'm all right.   I am just tired."

Then his senses cleared and his strength came back and he sat up and looked about.   The players of both teams were clustered around him, anxious and pale-faced.

"Thank Heaven, kid, that you didn't get killed," said Big Bill.   "That was a terrible blow.   It was old Manito that knocked the goal post down and hit you on the head as you went through. I guess you will be all right in a minute."

"What's all that yelling for over on our side?" asked Larry. "Did we score? Did we beat?"

"We sure did, kid," returned Bill, "it was you and Patches that did the trick. That hoss is a wonder and his rider is jest as good as he is."

Then the cow-punchers' supporters, a thousand strong, formed in marching order with the band leading and the polo team at their head and started uptown. Soon the cow-punchers who could not restrain their glee opened up with their .45's in a Fourth of July celebration. At first the shots were scattering, but soon they increased until there was a continuous roar which reminded the troopers of a miniature battle.

The band played Hail to the Chief, and The Conquering Hero Comes, and the cow-punchers sang We're Going Down to Old Wyanne, and Hurry Up You Little Dogie.

They marched and counter-marched through all the main streets and finally drew up before the city hall where each man of the polo team was obliged to make a speech.

It was not until the setting sun had touched the western Wyoming hills and long purple shadows began stealing across the fields behind the trees and fences that the party dispersed and the polo team and the rest of the Crooked Creek cow-punchers thought of home.

"This is going to be pretty tough on you, Larry" said Uncle Henry. "I never thought what a hard day you'd have when I made the arrangements. You see, we started the chuck wagon back this morning and our camp for tonight is thirty miles up the wagon trail towards home. There is over a hundred miles to make between now and to-morrow night where our Thanksgiving dinner will be served at eight o'clock and we must all be there."

Larry groaned inwardly and a great sigh escaped him. It seemed to him that he had never been so tired before in his entire life. Every muscle in his whole body was sore and his back ached so he could hardly sit in the saddle. His wrists were red and swollen and there was a big welt on the back of one hand.

"If you think it will be too much for you," continued his uncle, "we can stay over at a hotel, but the boys will be terribly disappointed if we don't get back for to-morrow night."

Then Larry pulled himself together. It was a strenuous country in which he was living and he was doing a man's part. These cow-punchers were like iron. Fatigue that would kill an ordinary man was nothing to them. Above everything else in the

world they admired fortitude.   He could not show
the white feather now, he would buck up.

"All right, Uncle Henry," he said.   "I guess I am
good for it. You hold Patches for a minute; I want
to go into this grocery store and make a purchase."

Five minutes later the young man re-appeared and
the weariness which had been so heavy upon him
seemed to have departed.   In that short time he had
pulled himself together and re-captured his fighting
spirit.

Then the little band of cow-punchers swung into
their saddles, gave a few departing war whoops, and
disappeared in a cloud of dust.   It must not be imagined that they kept up this wild gallop for long.   This
was just for its moral effect upon the citizens of
Wyanne. The members of the polo team were probably
four as tired and jaded men as could have been found
in the state of Wyoming on that night before Thanksgiving Day.

Once outside the town the ponies fell into their
habitual running walk, a gait as easy as the trot of
a fox and that eats up the miles like the lope of the
lobo wolf, a gait that is easy on both man and horse.

When they had covered about five miles Larry pulled
Patches up at a convenient turn in the trail which he
knew would hide them from sight. Here he dismounted and began feeling in his pockets.   Patches

thought he understood what his master was looking for and he began nosing about in the different pockets, helping in the search.   Finally he found one that bulged more than the rest and this held his attention.

"All right, old chum," said his master, "you've found it."   And he pulled out a small bag of lump sugar and gave one to Patches.   Patches crowded up close to him and was as excited about the sugar as a small boy would have been over a bag of candy.

"Now kiss me on the right cheek," said Larry and held a lump of sugar up against his cheek.   Patches reached over and, with his upper and lower lip, gently pinched his master's cheek and got the desired lump of sugar.

"Now kiss me on the other cheek," he said turning the left side of his face to Patches.   With the same gentle pinch he got another lump of sugar.

"Now make a bow and you get two."   Patches salaamed very low and got the desired lumps.

"Now shake hands for the next."   And Patches' fore foot went up.

"Now," said the boy, putting his arm around the horse's neck affectionately and laying his face against that of the faithful steed, "I'm going to tell you a secret. It wasn't me than won that polo game. It was you, do you know that?"   And Patches nickered knowingly. "Now you keep still a minute and don't fidget about and I'll tell you just how you did it. When I made that last shot I didn't hit the ball squarely and it wasn't quite through. You struck it with your foot and got the goal. Don't you see, you scored the winning goal?"

Patches whinnied and asked for another lump of sugar and got two for good measure. Then Larry smoothed out his fore top under the brow band and stroked his beautiful flowing mane, caressed his soft nose and gave him the remaining lumps of sugar.

"Come on, old pal," he said, "we got to be going. They must be a mile ahead of us."

So he swung into his saddle again and Patches resumed his steady lope. Three hours later the faithful horse was nibbling the frost-bitten grass by the roadside thirty miles from Wyanne while his master, wrapped in his blanket with his feet to the camp fire, slept the sleep of utter exhaustion.

CHAPTER VII

TWO TOES THE TERRIBLE

EARLY in December all of the help on the Crooked Creek ranch, with the exception of Hank Brodie and the polo team, were discharged and the men drifted away to seek other employment or to loaf during the winter and the ranch settled down into the quiet of the long cold winter.

Christmas was a very lively day at the ranch house. There was a Christmas tree for the children of the manager and the cow-punchers entered into this festivity with all the abandon of youth. In the evening there was an old-time country dance. Men and women came from neighboring ranches for fifty miles around. The furniture in the long narrow ranch room was stacked up in the hallway and in the corners of the room, and an old fashioned dance was enjoyed until the small hours of the morning with two squeaky violins and a portable organ to furnish the music. Long Tom in a high-keyed nasal voice called off the figures.

After this holiday dance there was little sociability or farm work until the spring time. By the first of

the year when the days began to lengthen and the cold
to strengthen, winter set in in earnest. Larry who had
been brought up in New England thought he knew
what snow was, but he soon found that he was mistaken.   For it fell out here in Wyoming day after
day in great white, shifting, drifting flakes which
piled up in enormous drifts.

With the coming of the deep snow the cow-punchers
got out what ponies had been kept in the corral and
began breaking out paths for the cattle.   A cow-
puncher mounted upon his favorite steed and leading
three other ponies behind him would make a path for
the cattle leading to the best feed and drinking places.
The parada had gradually drifted down to the lower
plateau and had taken refuge in several sheltered
canyons on some unfenced land below the plateau.
Here they were somewhat sheltered and the snow was
not so deep. The ponies, of which there were about
a hundred loose on the ranch, made better work of
feeding in the winter time than did the cows. They
would go from point to point pawing under the snow
and uncovering the seered, frost-bitten grass.   Each
pony was sure to have a string of cows following after
him to pick up the morsels that he left.

After the middle of January the hay stacks on the
home ranch, containing several hundred tons of hay,
were thrown open to the cattle.   They fell upon it

CHRISTMAS WAS A LIVELY DAY AT THE RANCH HOUSE

ravenously and it disappeared before their onset like dew before the sun. In another month they had eaten the last spear of hay and were still hungry. Then several tons of oilcake were brought out to tide them over for another few days. This was made of flax-seed ground and pressed into sheets. It was very nutritious and there was a saying among the cow-punchers that if a cow has been dead only twenty-four hours it will bring her round.

By the first of February the cold was intense and then the cattle were seen standing about forlornly. When Larry inquired the reason for this his uncle explained that they could stand the cold better by standing still; moving about against the wind might freeze them stiff in a few hours. Their coats which had been glossy and bright early in November were now dull and lusterless. Their ribs which had been covered with fat in early fall began to show through beneath the hide. Then it was that here and there over the panorama of white, small hillocks of snow were seen. When Larry poked into the first one he saw, he was horrified to find a dead cow beneath it. But he soon got used to this gruesome sight and it was a fortunate day when he did not discover a half dozen. Some of these cattle died from exposure and pneumonia and some starved to death, but this was expected on a great ranch where so many cattle were taken care of and the cow-punchers looked upon it as a part of the day's work.

Late in February when the sun had mounted higher in the heavens and its rays were warmer the snow would melt in sheltered spots on warm days. Then a very perceptible odor from these pathetic little piles of snow was noticed on the spring air.

It was to the call of such an allurement as this that Two Toes the Terrible led his band of seven grizzled hunters over the mountains that hemmed in the Crooked Creek ranch on the north and down onto the upper plateau. Two Toes was by far the most destructive wolf that had ever harassed the cattle growers of the northwest. In four states bounties were set upon his scalp by both county governments and private corporations. The aggregate of these bounties was fifteen hundred dollars so it will be well understood that the stock men wished to get rid of him. He had killed sheep by the thousands in South Dakota. He and his band would steal upon the sheep when they were bunched for the night and the shepherds were asleep and they would scatter before the onset of the wolves like chaff before the wind. Then for several days they would go about killing the small bands of unfortunate sheep. They had been known to kill as many as three hundred in a single night, while for the shepherd to find twenty or thirty terribly mangled sheep was a common thing. They never ate them, not caring for mutton, but merely killed them for the excitement of the chase.

Two Toes had killed calves and colts in Nebraska and had driven several horse-raisers who had ranches in southeastern Montana nearly to despair. In Wyoming he had killed calves and yearlings and done much damage on the cattle ranches. Although he never ate mutton he did like a tender young colt, but his favorite diet was calves and yearling heifers. He was so fastidious that he never ate an adult animal and as this band of wolves never ate anything that they did not kill themselves they were immune to all kinds of poison.

Old Two Toes' cunning in perceiving traps was almost beyond belief. His nose always warned him of danger and never was at fault. He would go where some trapper had set twenty-five to fifty steel traps for his little band and with diabolical cunning would discover each trap. Some of them he would uncover and these he would spring by scratching sticks or stones on them. Several government hunters, employed especially for the purpose, had camped on his trail for four or five years.

He was well-known to the biological branch of a certain department of the government in Washington. Just as a great city catalogs its crooks and keeps a gallery of them, so the Washington government keeps a catalog of the most destructive animals, and Two Toes' record was the most formidable in the department. It consisted of a long story of his ravages and several photographs of him which a government hunter had taken one day when he was armed with a telephoto instead of a rifle. There were also drawings of his peculiar track. Only once in his adventurous life had he ever fallen into a trap and then he had stumbled upon it in an out-of-the-way place when fleeing from an enemy. This misfortune had cost him the two middle toes on his right fore-foot and wherever he went he left the peculiar trail of this club foot. There were really two toes and a dewclaw on this foot, but the latter did not show in a dirt trail so he was usually referred to as Old Two Toes.

Before he had been on the Crooked Creek ranch for twenty-four hours, he and his band had killed half a dozen calves and three or four yearlings.

Hank Brodie had at once recognized that the ranch had some bad visitors and it was not many days before he discovered the peculiar trail of Old Two Toes; then he knew they were in for trouble.

He sent to the nearest drug store for a supply of arsenic and strychnine. All of the carcasses of the animals that had been killed were doctored with poison. He also cut pieces of meat from these carcasses and poisoned them using every precaution not to taint them. He likewise tried to tempt the wolves with freshly killed chickens dosing them in the same manner with the poison. But all his attempts to poison the wolves were futile, for they escaped the poisoned meat by leaving it rigidly alone. In some places they showed their contempt for this strategy by scratching snow and dirt over the meat and defiling it in other ways. Seeing it was useless to work further with the poison fifty new steel traps were secured and these were set in all the likely places. They were set in pairs and in threes, baited and unbaited, with all the skill that a local trapper who had been called in to help could devise. But day after day went by and no wolves were trapped, but the killing of calves and yearlings went steadily on. The wolves finally became so bold under Old Two Toes' leadership that they would come in close to the ranch house. No one ever saw them but their tracks left in the snow could plainly be seen the following morning.

One night Larry was awakened from a sound sleep by a most pitiful yelling from Billy, the Scotch collie, who was the only dog tolerated on the ranch. The outcries were so terrible that Larry sprang from his bed and hurried to the bunk house door, for the cries had seemed to come just outside. There on the door step he found the beautiful dog lying in the welter of his own blood and gasping for breath. But stranger even than that, Patches who was supposed to be safely housed in the corral was standing by his side and bending over him solicitously; for Patches and Billy were the greatest of friends. Billy always greeted Patches by jumping up and licking his nose when he and Larry came in from a ride over the ranch.

Larry picked Billy up gently and carried him into the bunk house and laid him on the rug inside the door. Then he called Hank Brodie and the rest of the cow-punchers. One glance at the dog was enough for them. They recognized the work of his assailants.

"It's wolves," said Long Tom, "and I guess they has done for Billy."

The prophecy was a good one for five minutes later the noble dog had breathed his last. Larry was heart-broken, but seeing he could do nothing more for Billy he put on his clothes and went outside to put Patches back in the corral again, but Patches was gone. He whistled and searched about the ranch buildings for half an hour but not a sign of the horse could he discover, and strangest of all the corral bars were up. Then he went sorrowfully back into the bunk house and told this additional news to the cow-punchers.

"I wouldn't worry about him," said Hank Brodie, "he's probably just strayed out, but what beats me is how he ever got out of the corral."

"He'll turn up all right in the morning, son," said Big Bill. "Don't you worry about Patches; if I ever saw an animal that was capable of taking care of himself, it is that hoss."

All that night Larry was haunted with dreams of Patches and the wolves. First the horse would be galloping wildly over the snow with a half dozen of the gray, gaunt destroyers at his heels trying to hamstring him. Then the scene would change and Patches would be backed up against a cliff surrounded by the gray marauders who sprang at his throat and tried to pull him down. Several times Larry awoke in a dripping sweat to find his heart beating like a trip-hammer. Finally he gave up trying to sleep and waited impatiently for the sound of the alarm clock in the bunk house. When it finally sounded he sprang out of bed with alacrity and hastily dressed. This was the first time during nearly a year that he had lived on the ranch that he had ever been awake when the alarm clock rang.

He hastened outside to see what he could learn of the tragic events of the night before. His uncle and Big Bill were already on the scene looking at the tracks in the snow. Larry could make little of these hiero-glyphics in the snow, but to experienced trailers like his uncle and Bill the story was as plain as the printed page in a book.

"You see, it was this here way," said Bill when he had examined all the tracks carefully, "Old Two Toes was snooking about the place and surprised Billy and fell upon him like a thunder bolt, but Billy managed to ward him off for a few seconds by leaping about and dodging. But finally the old killer got the death grip, then it was that Billy set up that unearthly yelling and you couldn't blame him.

"Patches was probably the first one to hear this call of his friend for help and he went over the corral fence like a rocket although it is seven feet high. He fell on that Old Two Toes like a ton of brick and the old killer suddenly remembered that he had very urgent business in another part of the ranch and he lit out for parts unknown going about twelve feet at a jump and Patches after him. But after the first hundred feet or two Patches turned back to see how Billy was and escorted him to the bunk house steps. When he saw you had taken his chum inside, he again went after the wolf."

Immediately after breakfast Hank Brodie and Larry saddled their horses and started out to find the truant Patches. Larry was mounted upon the Jack Rabbit which Pony had loaned for the occasion.

They were able to follow the tracks of the wolves and the horse for about two miles, until Old Two Toes took to the timber. Here Patches was joined by some other horses and his track could not be told from the rest of the herd.

Larry and his uncle rode hither and yon over the ranch and it was not until about four o'clock in the afternoon that they caught sight of Patches. And then they found him standing upon a swell on the upper plateau, away to the north over close to the perimeter of the mountains. He seemed to be gazing intently across the snow and almost immediately Hank Brodie saw three other horses standing upon nearby swells, all in this watchful attitude. Larry was overjoyed to see his chum and at once started after him using the shrill whistle that he always employed when he wished to call the horse. But to his great surprise when he came within about sixty yards of his chum Patches threw up his head and galloped off and they saw him no more that day.

"Well," said Hank Brodie, "I guess we've lost him for this time but we'll get him to-morrow."

Larry was loathe to give up the pursuit, but finally seeing that his uncle was right he reluctantly turned back to the ranch house.

Early the following morning they were out on the range again looking for Patches. This time they were more successful in locating him and discovered him about noon. But he was still as wary as he had been the day before. He would allow Larry to approach

within fifty yards, then he would throw up his head
and trot away. The boy followed him for hours thinking he would wear out this persistent aloofness, but
all to no purpose. When night fell he was still as
far from securing his horse chum as ever.

"Don't be discouraged, son" said Big Bill to him
that night as he recounted the day's futile pursuit,
"when he gets good and ready he will let you catch
him. Until then there ain't much use chasing him.
I'd jest let him alone."

But Larry could not content himself with idleness
and every day for two weeks he went out to look for
Patches. Some days he didn't see the horse at all and
then a great fear would seize him. Perhaps he had
ventured into the timber and the wolves had pulled
him down. But the following day Larry would usually
find him.

It seemed to Larry that the brightest and best thing
in his life had been taken from him. He never could
have imagined he would miss a mere animal so terribly. But Patches was more than an animal; he
was a chum, a companion in the day's work. He and
Larry had ranged the ranch together early and late,
in spring, summer, autumn, and winter and they had
come to be inseparable. If Patches missed Larry he
gave no sign for at the end of two weeks he still
eluded him just as he had the first day.

One evening before sundown Larry went to the top
of the pinnacle above Piñon Valley where his uncle
had taken him on that memorable day when he had
shown him "the cattle on a thousand hills."

Larry scanned the country through his glass for a
long time before he made out anything that interested
him.   But finally he discovered on the upper plateau
a dog-like animal trotting towards the cul-de-sac or
neck of the bottle which led through into Piñon Valley.

At first he thought it was surely an enormous dog,
then as the animal drew nearer he saw to his great
surprise that it was a gigantic wolf, perhaps Two Toes
himself.

Larry's surprise on discovering the wolf had barely
subsided when he noticed a horse following about
seventy-five yards behind the wolf, but he was not
alone for presently Larry discovered nearly a dozen
other horses all spread out in an elliptical shape behind the wolf, and then he saw that the horse leading
was Patches.

Then Larry noticed that the great wolf seemed very
tired, for he trotted wearily along and not with the
usual springy lope of the lobo wolf.

But soon he lost him as he disappeared in the neck
of the bottle.   He turned his glass upon the point
where he must reappear at the upper end of Piñon
Valley.

Presently he saw him come trotting wearily forth. He had not covered more than a third of the distance through the valley when Patches and his little band of horses broke out of the cul-de-sac. When Larry had last seen them they had been trotting leisurely but now they broke into a wild gallop and swept down the valley upon the solitary wolf like a whirlwind.

Larry thought he had seen range horses run before but he had never seen such running as he now beheld on the part of this little flying squadron. They gained steadily upon the wolf who looked back once and saw the on-coming menace. He seemed to appreciate his danger for he put forth his utmost strength and ran belly to earth, but even so the flying squadron of riderless cavalry gained on him. When about half way down the valley Old Two Toes turned to the left to escape, if possible, in the piñons and junipers upon the steep hillside. But Patches who was leading that wing of the charging herd let out a great burst of speed and quickly headed the gray wolf back to the center of the valley. Then the beleaguered wolf tried the right side but this wing of Patches' little troop of cavalry increased its speed and headed him back. Slowly the two jaws of this phalanx of pounding hoofs were closing in upon him. Again he tried the straight away run down the valley but the flying horses increased their speed. Once the wolf hesitated and

THE HORSES GAINED STEADILY ON THE WOLF

looked, first this way and that for an escape and this hesitation was his undoing, for closing up their ranks the squadron passed over him like an express train and left him limp upon the snow. About fifty yards beyond the prostrate wolf, they wheeled as though by command of unseen riders and charged back. By this time the wolf had raised upon his fore-legs but his hind quarters seemed paralyzed and once again the charging horses passed over him.

Larry's heart gave a throb of fear as he saw the mighty wolf spring at Patches' throat but the pounding hoofs crushed him to earth and the flying broncho passed by unscathed. Once again the maneuvering squadron paused about fifty yards from the prostrate wolf, but this time Patches went back alone. He came up close to the fallen destroyer and reared upon his hind legs and brought down his forefeet like pile drivers upon the wolf. This he repeated thrice; then, concluding that all life had been crushed out of him, he returned to his little band.

Larry waited to see no more but made all haste down through the piñons and junipers, sending snow and sand sliding down before him. He reached Piñon Valley excited and breathless.

He found Patches and his little band of mustangs still bunched together just as he had last seen them. He thrust two fingers into his mouth and blew the shrill whistle with which he had called Patches so many times in days gone by. And this time to his great joy his chum nickered and trotted eagerly toward him while the rest of the mustangs galloped away in the direction from which they had come.

Patches seemed overjoyed to be with his master once more and immediately began nosing about his pockets for the bag of lump sugar that Larry had been carrying for the entire two weeks and which he had held up for Patches' inspection whenever he came near him. Patches ate a couple of lumps, kissed his master upon each cheek and bowed low. He got two more lumps and then he had to shake hands. From his manner it was apparent to Larry that the horse had lost none of his affection for him; he had simply been upon other business during the strange two weeks.

When Larry had petted him to his heart's content and Patches had eaten the last lump of sugar in the bag, Larry took the bridle and saddle from Baldy who had been hitched in the piñons nearby and put them on Patches. He put the halter that he had carried on his saddle bow for the past two weeks upon Baldy. Then by means of his lariat he bound the lobo wolf to Baldy's back. The old mustang objected at first but finally decided to carry the load. When the wolf had been made secure Larry mounted Patches and leading Baldy started triumphantly back to the ranch.

That evening by the long table in the ranch house he told the story to an excited audience. He told it well, not omitting any of the high-lights in Patches' performance. When he had finished Big Bill brought his fist down upon the table with a blow that made the dishes rattle.

"By heaven, gents, it is jest as I thought," he said. "I knowed it all the time but I reckon it is easier to prophesy after a thing is over that it is before it happens, but I knowed it jest the same.

"That air Patches has been camping on the trail of that old lobo wolf these two weeks. Whenever he came out in the open, he and his hosses were right after him a-wearing him down and pestering the life out'n him. They were waiting for the right opening to come and when he trotted into Piñon Valley he was as good as dead.

"Don't ever tell me again that a hoss ain't got some reasoning power. I knowed they have and they've got hoss sense besides, and that's more than some folks got."

When they came to weigh and measure the lobo wolf all the cow-punchers were amazed at his dimensions, for he stood thirty-five inches at his shoulders and weighed one hundred and forty-two pounds. When we remember that a large timber wolf only weighs about ninety pounds it will be seen that Two Toes was a giant among his fellows. The loss of their leader immediately demoralized the band of gray hunters and they were seen no more on the Crooked Creek ranch, and Patches got the credit of ridding the ranch of these destroyers.

CHAPTER VIII

OLD EPHRAIM

OLD Ephraim should have stayed in Yellowstone Park where he was well off, but like many humans he became dissatisfied with his lot and sought his fortunes in other regions and so came to grief. In the park he was protected by the government, with plenty of forage on the dumps of the many tourists' hotels, and, if he took a notion, he could kill an elk calf, for elk were very plentiful in the park being protected just as Old Ephraim was. But he failed to appreciate all of his blessings and so came into our story.

Old Ephraim was the facetious name which hunters and frontiersmen in the west had given to the Rocky Mountain grizzly bear. Before the discovery of the great Kodiak bear on Kodiak Island in Alaska it was thought that the Rocky Mountain grizzly was king among carnivorous animals in the western hemisphere, but the discovery of the Kodiak bear took this palm from him.

Old Ephraim at the time of our story was five or six years old and while he was not of record-breaking size yet he was most formidable. Six or seven hundred pounds of bear meat armed with death-dealing paws and prodigious claws are about as much bear as even a brave man would want to see coming after him unless he was heavily armed.

Old Ephraim had come from his hibernation about April first. He had been fat in autumn when he had begun the long winter sleep, but now his coat was dull and lifeless. His flesh had disappeared and his digestive organs were also at a low ebb. So for the first ten days after coming forth from his long winter's sleep he ate little but grasses and roots, leaving his digestive organs to recover their vigor. Then it was that the blood-lust came upon him. Even so he might have satisfied it with an elk calf but that was not to his liking. He remembered the year before having tasted mutton and now a great desire to feed upon that delicacy came over him. So one April morning he left the park and pointed his nose to the southeast and started on his long journey. He was very lucky in his quest for sheep and discovered a small sheep ranch towards the close of the first day. Like a good hunter he waited until after dark and then fell on the flock and killed several sheep and so satisfied his longing for mutton and warm blood. He was not like Two Toes the Terrible, killing merely for the excitement of the chase for Old Ephraim killed to satisfy his appetite.

The following day he found more meat for he discovered a mule deer which had broken a fore-leg in a windfall. She was quite at his mercy and he broke her neck with a terrific left-hand blow from his great paw, for most bears are left handed.

The third day of his peregrinations he found a convenient stream where trout and suckers were very plentiful and he spent the better part of the day fishing. He would crouch upon a flat stone close to the stream and whenever a fish came to the surface to snap up a fly that had fallen upon the water, with one stroke of his great paw he would knock the fish out upon the land and eat it at his leisure.

On the fourth day of his travels he discovered a bee-tree and had the time of his life driving out the owners of the sweet and possessing himself of the results of many months of toil. He did not mind that he got stung upon his nose and lips for the delicious honey well repaid him for the smart of the bee stings.

The fifth day he crossed the mountains above Crooked Creek ranch and came down into Aspen Draw, a little gulch close to the timber above the upper mesa and Piñon Valley.

Here the following day he killed a yearling heifer and so his presence upon the ranch became known. Larry was the one who discovered the kill as he was doing most of the range riding. He examined the carcass to the best of his ability but he did not have the trained eyes of a woodsman, so failed to note all the signs. One thing he was sure of, it was probably not the work of the wolves for nothing had been seen of the gray pack since the loss of Old Two Toes.

When he conducted his uncle, Hank Brodie, to the spot, this veteran trailer at once pointed out the large track in the soft dirt close to the heifer. It was as large as the palm of a man's hand with the fingers outspread. At the perimeter of the track were five large claw prints.

"What do you make of that, son?" inquired Hank Brodie pointing to the unmistakable sign.

"Whew," returned Larry, "how did I ever overlook that? He must be a whopper whatever he is."

"It is Old Ephraim," his uncle returned. "That is the frontier name for the great Rocky Mountain grizzly. We certainly got an important visitor this time, but we will wait and see what he will do. I don't think he will be as bad as the wolves."

But Old Ephraim was hungry and the Crooked Creek calves and yearlings tasted good to him so he killed a fresh one every day. Finally Hank Brodie had to see what he could do with traps.

So three or four of the cow-punchers set out one day with axes to build a pen trap. They built it on the edge of the timber close to Piñon Valley. It was made of lodge-pole pines about ten inches in diameter. These were notched at the ends and the corners were locked together just as the old time log cabin was built. Poles were put across the top of the pen, when the sides were completed, to make a roof and heavy stones were laid upon them to make the roof secure. Then a log door was built and this was held up by a strong rope which passed over the roof of the house and down the backside and through the wall to the trigger inside. When everything was in readiness the trap was baited with a freshly killed calf's head and the cow-punchers went home to await developments.

For two days Old Ephraim did not seem to discover the pen trap but on the third night he entered it and pulled the trigger and the door went down with a great bang. Judging from the appearance of the house the next day, the mighty grizzly had been infuriated on being entrapped in this way. He had evidently reared to his full height and placing his strong shoulders against the roof had literally lifted the poles and the boulders upon them and thrown them to the ground. He had done a very thorough job in demolishing the pen trap for he had not only stripped off the entire roof but he had also torn out one side of the trap. Evidence of his fury could be seen where he had stripped the bark from the lodge-poles leaving great claw marks, some of them a foot long.

"That old paw would make a man sick if he ever raked it down his back," said Uncle Hank as he pointed to the signs of Old Ephraim's fury.

Hank next tried a deadfall. He secured a log about fifteen feet long and drove down stakes each side of it until he had made a lane with the log in the middle of it. Then one end was raised to the height of perhaps eight feet and held in place by means of a figure four. On the spindle of the figure four was placed a frame of honey which a cow-puncher had ridden twenty miles to secure.

Old Ephraim evidently was suspicious of this deadfall for he did not go very near it for a day or two, but finally the honey became too much for him. Even then he did not venture into the lane under the deadfall but pulled up several stakes at the sides and then thrust his arm in and secured the honey without injury to himself although the deadfall was sprung.

Hank next tried a half dozen of the heavy steel traps that he had used for the wolves. Old Ephraim finally blundered into two of them, but he merely took the log to which they were fastened on his shoulder and carrying it to the nearest tree had beaten the traps against it until they came to pieces. Parts of them were seen strewn on the ground.

This last failure discouraged Hank Brodie and he did not try further to catch the big bear, but tried poison instead. He put arsenic and strychnine into pieces of meat near each kill when it was found, but Old Ephraim's nose could not be deceived and he always let poisoned meat strictly alone.

There is no telling how long the grizzly would have remained on the Crooked Creek ranch had not an unforeseen meeting taken place, one which gave all parties participating considerable surprise.

Larry and Patches had been riding on the upper mesa looking for spring calves and had just ridden into Aspen Draw, when, as they neared a fringe of bushes at the side of the canyon, Patches suddenly snorted and became very excited and pranced about. Larry was much astonished as he had never seen him act like this before but the fear of the horse was immediately explained. For the next instant a mighty grizzly bear reared on his haunches and looked over the tops of the bushes at the horse and rider. He was not over forty feet away and to Larry he looked a veritable mountain. Hank Brodie had cautioned the boy against shooting at the grizzly if he should ever come upon him at close range for he might infuriate him and precipitate trouble.

Larry forgot this warning and instinctively his hand slid to his six gun, and, before he could formulate a plan of escape, he had raised his revolver and fired. The bullet struck the bear a glancing blow upon the shoulder which did no damage, but threw Old Ephraim into a towering rage.

With a roar of pain and fury the old grizzly charged straight at the horse and rider. Now while a grizzly bear is rather slow in a straight away run, in a sudden charge he can often put forth a great burst of speed which almost approaches that of the mountain lion.

And this was what Old Ephraim did. He had been attacked without provocation and he intended that somebody should smart for it. Before Larry had time to tighten the line in his left hand the bear had taken two jumps. Then in the excitement Larry dropped his .45 and clutched the quirt and brought it down on Patches' side. The horse wheeled partly about as though to run and then seemed to change his mind, or perhaps he was rooted to the ground with fear. Anyhow he did not break into the wild gallop Larry had expected. Instead he stood rigidly, his forefeet planted like pile drivers and Larry felt the horse's muscles beneath the saddle grow tense. Patches, looking back over his shoulder, timed his attack just as a baseball player swings his bat to meet the flying ball. So when the great grizzly executed his fourth jump, which would have carried him upon the horse's flank, Patches lashed out with both heels in a terrific kick which hit the bear squarely. One hoof struck the side of his neck, and the other caught him beneath the jaw. Larry heard

THE OLD GRIZZLY CHARGED STRAIGHT AT THE HORSE AND RIDER

something break, which sounded like breaking wood, and the thought flashed through his mind that Patches had broken his own leg. The recoil from the kick was terrific, and it threw Patches forward upon his knees; while Larry went flying over the horse's head striking on his own head and shoulders on the ground. For two or three seconds he seemed to lose consciousness and a faint sick feeling gripped him and everything was dark. But almost immediately his vitality reasserted itself, and his mind cleared. He raised to a sitting position only to see, not ten feet away, a mighty grizzly also struggling to his feet. He was working his jaw and winking his eyelids. He seemed as dazed as Larry himself and very much bewildered about what had happened.

For a moment Larry was paralyzed with fear, then he remembered his six gun and his hand went to the holster, but it was empty. Just at this moment he noticed that he was kneeling upon something hard and looking down he discovered his revolver half buried in the dirt. Frantically he clutched it and without realizing what the results might be, fired the remaining five shots in quick succession into the great bear. Then seeing that his gun was useless, in a fit of frenzy, he threw the revolver with all his might at the bear's head and ran for his life.

In the New England high school which Larry had attended he had been considered something of a sprinter. He had run one-hundred yards in ten and three-fifths seconds, which is very fast for a high school boy. But he never ran on the track under a watch as he now fled down Aspen Draw. It seemed to him with every jump that the great bear was close upon him and he began zigzagging this way and that thinking by so doing he might escape the mighty paw of his pursuer. Once he imagined he could even feel the hot breath of the great beast upon his back.

By the time he had covered one-hundred yards his breath came in gasps, but he could not stop or slacken his speed. At the end of one hundred and fifty yards his breath was coming in a wheezy whistle. He had to slacken his pace for a second to breathe, so he looked back for his pursuer, but to his surprise there was no bear in sight. He stood for about ten seconds gazing back up the draw, but there was no grizzly on his track. But this did not hinder him making all haste to Patches, who was waiting for him another fifty yards down the draw. With what remaining strength Larry had he climbed into the saddle and putting spurs to the horse he galloped back to the ranch house. Pony was the only cow-puncher that he could find at the ranch house, and he, at first, greeted Larry's story with shouts of derision and laughter. But, finally, seeing how much in earnest the boy was and discovering that Patches had skinned one of his knees he saddled the Jack Rabbit and together they returned to Aspen Draw.

They approached the spot where Larry had last seen Old Ephraim, with drawn revolvers, but this precaution was entirely unnecessary for they found on drawing near that the great bear was lying on the ground motionless where Larry had last seen him.

They took the precaution to throw stones at him before they approached very near, but finally discovered that he was quite lifeless. Careful examination of the grizzly showed that Patches' terrific kick had dislocated his neck and broken his lower jaw, while five of Larry's bullets had taken effect. This was quite enough for one bear so it was no wonder Old Ephraim was dead.

By the light of two lanterns and the May moon they skinned the grizzly and after cutting out twenty pounds of bear steak they took the skin and the steak home and left the remainder for the coyotes.

That evening as they sat about the supper table, Larry told the story in detail. And it was Big Bill who summed up the sentiments of the company.

"That air hoss, Patches," said the big fellow, accenting his remarks with a blow on the table, "is a wonder. He is the all-fired'st hoss I ever heard of. He bagged that old Two Toes when government hunters had been after him for five years. Now he has bagged the grizzly. If that ain't some doings for a hoss."

"That hoss is worth a thousand dollars in gold," put in Pony.

"He is worth more than that," said Larry stoutly. "I wouldn't sell him for all the money in Wyoming."

CHAPTER IX

THE INVADERS

IF there was one subject which fascinated Larry above all else, it was the cattle industry. He was never tired of hearing about it, and on warm summer evenings, when it was too hot to play polo, his uncle and the rest of the cow-punchers would stretch out on the grass under a big cottonwood near the ranch house and spin yarns of the cattle business. Such old timers as Big Bill, Long Tom, and Pony could by the hour recite tales of the old days; days of the Gilson and Santa Fe trails; of desperate fights between rival ranchmen in New Mexico and on the Panhandle. In addition to that there was the endless strife between the cattle men and the sheep men. If there was one individual in the whole world that a cattle man despised above all others it was a shepherd, and he in turn despised a goat man. Large herds of goats, however, were rarely seen in Wyoming.

Then in addition to these natural foes the cattle men had always had to fight the homesteaders, especially that drifting portion of homesteaders known as floaters or nesters. And worst of all there was the rustler, an

173

unscrupulous scoundrel who fattened upon other people's labors and reaped where he had not sown.

In addition to all of these menaces to the cattle industry there were the wolves and the bears, not to mention the coyotes who were not really a serious menace.

Many of the battles which the cattle men waged with their human foes were fought over the water holes, for water was most important in both the cattle and the sheep industries.

In the very early days of the industry good grazing land had been so plenty that it was not worth fighting for. In those glorious old days a cattle man had been a king indeed and he ruled with an iron hand, but gradually the homesteader had driven him farther and farther west. He had seen the best grazing land set apart by the government for homesteading and his own despotic power had gradually waned.

Up to the early '90's, however, he had been king, and no one had really questioned his authority for he always backed up his claims with force. But things had come to a head one spring morning in the early '90's when about two hundred cow-punchers, armed to the teeth, had met an equal number of sheriffs composed of homesteaders and their sympathizers. The cow-punchers had come out to eject some homesteader from land which they thought they owned. The two little armies had been drawn up face to face and a desperate encounter would have ensued had not a troop of United States cavalry intervened. This blow by the homesteaders had broken the power of the cattle men for all time.

The setting of this stirring drama of the cattle business was certainly picturesque; the broad prairies with their thousands of acres of bunch grass, the low-lying land with its bluejoint, and even the timber land where the juicy pine grass grew so plentifully, were all a veritable wonderland. It was no wonder that the cowpunchers should spin such yarns with such a background.

So, while Larry knew all the history and the tradition of the cattle business and all of its theories, yet he often found that in practice there were many exceptions to these theories and often difficulties and problems arose which he had never dreamed of.

For instance, he had never imagined that he would live to see a flock of sheep on the Crooked Creek ranch, or that they would be subjected to the menace of floaters or nesters, or even more unthinkable than either of these possibilities was the probability that they would ever suffer from rustlers, yet all three of these unforeseen possibilities came to pass under his very eyes.

One morning about the first of June, Larry had been sent by his uncle into the unfenced land of the Crooked Creek ranch which lay to the southeast. There were thousands of acres there which were used by the cow-punchers only during the winter time. It was not very good grassland for it was rather sandy and rugged, being broken with many draws and buttes, but in the winter time it was sheltered and the cattle often weathered a long hard storm in these friendly little canyons.

Hank Brodie had told his nephew to ride over the country and see how it looked and if there were any signs of nesters. It must not be imagined, however, that this territory was entirely devoid of grassland for there were several small intervales of fifty or a hundred acres each where there was good feeding.

Larry's astonishment can well be imagined, when on approaching the largest of these intervales, he found it fairly white with sheep. There were not only hundreds of them, but it seemed to Larry that there were thousands and tens of thousands, although there really were only three thousand. But in every direction as far as his eyes could reach, the grassland was white with sheep. Knowing of the hostility between the cattle men and the sheep men, Larry did not approach any of the three or four shepherds that he saw with the sheep, but contented himself with reconnoitering from a distance. When he had secured all the information that he wanted he returned in hot haste to report to his uncle.

As Larry had expected, his uncle was thrown into consternation by the news, but lost no time in bewailing the fact. He went at once to the corral to saddle his horse.

"You'll have to come along with me, Larry," he said, "I don't just like to take you on such an errand, but there don't seem to be anyone else around and I want a witness."

Larry was not altogether surprised when he saw his uncle buckle on two .45's. He also insisted on inspecting Larry's own gun.

"We probably won't have to use them this time, but it is always best to be prepared. These sheep men are the scum of the earth," said his uncle.

Half an hour later they arrived at the intervale where Larry had found the large herd of sheep and Hank Brodie saw that his nephew had given a faithful report of the conditions. There were four shepherds in charge, and the head cow-puncher of the Crooked Creek ranch at once sought out the foreman of the shepherds.

"What in the devil are you and your stinking sheep doing on my land?" thundered Hank.

"It ain't your land any more than its our'n," returned the shepherd coolly. "It belongs to the government and what belongs to them is as much our'n as it's your'n."

"It doesn't belong to the government," returned Hank, vigorously, "We've grazed it for twenty years and it belongs to us and there ain't no stinking sheep men going to take it away from us."

"Have you got a deed to it?" sneered the shepherd.

"That's my business," returned Hank. "It is ours, I tell you, and you have got to get out."

"We have looked up the titles down at Wyanne and it ain't no more yours than it's our'n. Here we are and here we stay," returned the shepherd.

Although Larry had heard much of the strenuousness of the cattle men and their domination of the land, yet he was amazed at his uncle's next words. He was usually a quiet-spoken man with a pleasing voice, though now it became ominous and his words were hissed through partly set teeth. To Larry it seemed that the two men as they glared at each other were like two savage beasts fighting over some recent kill. And that is just what it really was, it was a case of primeval man asserting by force his right to the land.

"This is my last word to you," hissed Hank Brodie between his teeth. "We've got ten good cow-punchers up at the Crooked Creek ranch and they all own a .45 and some of them tote two. We've got four or five Winchesters kicking around also. We're coming down here to-morrow morning at sunup and if any of you stinking sheep men are around, we'll shoot you so full of holes that you won't be able to cast a shadow. Now take your choice, go or stay."

With this threat Hank wheeled Baldy sharply about and galloped away and his nephew had nothing to do but follow. When they had gone half a mile Hank pulled Old Baldy down to a trot and allowed Larry to come alongside.

"I ought not to get you into such a fuss as this," he said. "I should have taken one of the old hands along with me. Don't let it bother you, boy."

"Will you and the rest of the boys come down here tomorrow morning and shoot them full of holes as you said?" inquired Larry incredulously.

In spite of the seriousness of the situation Hank laughed.

"Well, it probably won't come to that. If they really stick it out we may shoot their boot heels off and stampede their sheep into Crooked Creek, but we probably won't kill any of them. We won't worry about tomorrow until tomorrow comes."

There was great excitement that evening at supper time when Hank told of the encounter and the cow-punchers of the Crooked Creek ranch were very indignant and ready to back up the head cow-puncher at any cost.

The following morning when Larry awoke, he found the bunk house empty. The alarm clock had not gone off. Old Bill had purposely turned the alarm off, and he and the rest of the men had tip-toed silently out an hour before. Larry dressed in great haste wondering what was up until he remembered the encounter with the sheep men and his uncle's threat. He hurried outside but could not find any of his brother cow-punchers. The ranch house, the saddle shed, the corral, and the stables were all deserted and an ominous silence reigned.

When he asked Mrs. Morgan what had become of the cow-punchers, she seemed strangely non-committal. So there was nothing to do but to wait developments. Larry got a book and sat under a friendly cottonwood, awaiting the return of the cow-punchers. Soon he heard them coming up the wagon trail at a brisk gallop. As they drew near he heard them laughing and jesting. They seemed in good spirits.

"It's all right, son," shouted Hank as they galloped into the yard. "The bluff worked. There ain't a sheep to be seen anywhere in the lowlands this morning. We called their bluff good and proper and they just lit out."

About a month after the discovery of the sheep men in the lowlands below Crooked Creek ranch Larry made another discovery for it was he who was doing most of the range riding. This time he found some nesters in the intervales where he had discovered the sheep men. They must have been there for some time for they had erected a two-room log cabin, a small horse corral, and a cow corral. It looked as though they intended to stay for they had made themselves quite at home and had chopped a large pile of cord wood. They had helped themselves very generously to cottonwood and lodge-pole pines both in the construction of their corrals and cabin and for the wood pile.

Larry did not go very near their new neighbors but contented himself with reconnoitering through his field glass. He finally made out that there were eight in the family, the father, the mother, and five boys, three of whom were nearly man-grown, and a small girl perhaps eight years of age with whom Larry afterwards became quite friendly.

The new interloper was one Fritz Ganzer, an alien of German extraction. Life had become too cramped for him in the homeland and he had sought his fortunes in the new world. He had been victimized by some land sharks down at Wyanne. He imagined that he had bought a quarter section and thought that he could homestead another quarter section, making three hundred and twenty acres in all. This amount of land he had preëmpted.

When Larry reported to his uncle, the latter seemed much surprised.

"The sheep men were bad enough," he commented, "but this German will be worse. If a German once gets an idea in his head, there is no getting it out."

Hank Brodie never told Larry just what he intended

to do and he was so slow in making the first move that his nephew thought he had forgotten about the floaters.

But one evening shortly after dark, without warning, the Ganzer family were suddenly attacked by eight or ten Indians, or at least they looked like Indians. They were generously smeared with war paint, wore sumptuous headdresses, and gorgeous blankets, and their feet were clad in moccasins, and they yelled in true redskin style.

The Ganzer family retreated to their cabin and replied in a desultory manner to the hail of bullets which spattered upon the chimney of their cabin and splintered the door posts, but did no other harm. During the melée the bars of the corral were let down and the two horses and the three cows were driven away. They were not lost permanently, but were found the following day two or three miles down Crooked Creek.

The ruse might have worked had it not been for an unfortunate episode in the attack. One of the redskin's horses was killed by a lucky shot from the little German and the rider fled in haste.

The Ganzer family found on examining the dead horse the following morning that he bore the tell-tale C C R with the encircling barbed wire fence which was the brand of the Crooked Creek ranch.

The next morning a little after sunup the little German accompanied by three of his stalwart sons appeared at the ranch house. He was very angry and sputtered away in his broken English.

"Vot in the tevil do you mean? You dress up your cow-puncher men like Indians and you come down to my place and you shoot up my ranch. I vant to be a good neighbor. I am a good man. I vant to live in America and I vant to farm this land and you do this bad thing. Vot you mean?"

"I'm not quite sure what you mean," replied Hank Brodie. "You will have to explain more fully if you want me to understand."

"Last night, me and my vife, Gretchen, and my boys, we were all eating supper when bang, bang, a lot of Indians ride out of the woods and they shoot and shoot and take down my bars and drive away my horse and my cow. Vot you mean by that?"

"You say they were Indians. I don't know anything about any Indians. It must have been some of the Sioux from the reservation. They get filled up with fire water once in a while and go on a rampage. You had better look out for they may sweep down on you some night and scalp you and your family."

"I tell you they was not Indians. It was your cow-puncher men who make up like Indians and try to drive away my cow."

"I don't know anything about any Indians," replied

Hank Brodie. "You will have to look elsewhere. Go to the government, they have charge of the Indians."

But the little German could not be placated. The more Hank talked the angrier he got and the more he railed in his broken English. Finally he left but with this threat.

"I vill get even with you, Mr. Cow-puncher Man. You think you shoot up my place and drive me out of the country. But this country belongs to me as much as to you. Your government man down at Wyanne he told me so. You try to keep all of the land but I vill keep vot I got and I vill get even with you."

Although there was no further immediate hostility between the family of Fritz Ganzer and the Crooked Creek ranch, yet bad blood between the two factions continued.

A couple of weeks after this interview the German's big police dog wandered up on the ranch and was shot by the cow-punchers. This was really not an act against the German for the cow-punchers always made it a rule to shoot stray dogs thinking they would frighten the calves. But Fritz interpreted the deed as a further act of war upon him and his family.

A week or two later while the Ganzer family were peacefully sleeping the bars of their corral were once more let down and the stock driven away. This time it took them half a day to recover it.

But no matter what the cow-punchers of the Crooked Creek ranch did to the family of the little German they still stayed by their guns and went on with their preparations for homesteading.

Just what form his revenge upon the Crooked Creek ranch would have taken is problematical had not nature played into his hands. The summer was a very dry one. There had been no rain for weeks. The feed upon the ranch which was usually of the best became brown and crisp. Leaves upon some of the trees even curled up. The land which was usually well watered became thirsty as a dry sponge and all the ranch especially the lower plateau was like a tinder box.

Under such conditions as these one can well imagine the consternation into which the cow-punchers were thrown one morning about the middle of July when one of their number came galloping in from the lower plateau shouting that the mesa was on fire in half a dozen places.

The lower plateau was perhaps four miles long and two miles wide. Crooked Creek which came down through Piñon Valley from the mountains above, skirted it on two sides and then continued on its way into the lowlands. Hank Brodie at once marshalled his little army to fight the fire and to extricate the six thousand head of badly frightened cattle from the dilemma in which they had been placed. The fire had apparently been kindled with diabolical skill so as to entrap the herd. It was later learned that Fritz Ganzer and one of his boys had been seen to leave the mesa that very morning and several brands which had been used in kindling the fires were afterward discovered.

Pandemonium reigned on the mesa. Calves and yearlings were dashing about with tails up while the younger cows were greatly excited over their calves.

It was so dry that great clouds of dust rose above the excited herd and this, added to the dense clouds of smoke, obscured the summer sun. Hank saw at once by acting quickly that the better part of the herd could be driven into Piñon Valley and thence to the upper plateau. But the cattle were not as tractable as usual; they were unreasonable and the cow-punchers had great difficulty in making them go in the right direction. It was desperate work for the air was filled with smoke and dust and since the sun and the distant mountains were hidden from sight they were not always sure of the direction. After half an hour of desperate work they had managed to pilot four thousand head safely into Piñon Valley and start them on the way to the upper plateau. But the other two thousand head seemed trapped. The narrow strip of grass along which they had driven the rest of the parada was now burning-feverishly.

Hank Brodie at once sized up the situation. There

IT WAS DESPERATE WORK FOR THE AIR WAS FILLED
WITH SMOKE AND DUST

was but one thing to do and he at once gave the order. "Cut the fence along Crooked Creek and stampede the rest of the herd across Crooked Creek into the timber on the side of the mountain."

The head cow-puncher knew very well that this was a dangerous thing to do for if the fire ever jumped the creek and caught the tall trees on the steep slopes the forest would prove a veritable fire trap, but it was the only chance so they shouted and waved their camp blankets at the cattle until they got them started across Crooked Creek. And none too soon for when the last head had crossed the river the cow-punchers themselves had to ride for their lives to escape the flames.

But the fire did its work very quickly and in two hours from the time it was first discovered it had spent its fury and only a smoldering ember here and there told of how fiercely the flames had burned an hour before. As soon as the earth would permit of the passage of cattle over it the two thousand head on the side of the mountain were driven back over Crooked Creek and headed for Piñon Valley and thence to the upper plateau. It was sundown when the parada of the Crooked Creek ranch had finally been made secure.

A madder set of cow-punchers than Hank Brodie's men could hardly have been found in Wyoming as they came in. Their expletives against Fritz Ganzer and his family were picturesque and wholly outside the domain of print.

Immediately after supper the cow-punchers saddled their broncs and started to interview the German. Hank insisted that they leave their guns behind and he himself carried but one which he had concealed under his vest. They intended to make a thorough job of the Ganzer family this time and run them out of the country.

But the wary little German had foreseen this move and when they arrived at the cabin they found it forsaken. He had driven away his horses and cattle and moved all his furniture and they saw every evidence that he had left the country for good, so the cow-punchers returned to the ranch house without wreaking their vengeance upon the man who had so nearly destroyed the parada of the ranch, but this much had been accomplished, they had apparently got rid of him for the present.

CHAPTER X

THE TRAGEDY

THE third invasion of the Crooked Creek ranch and the one Larry had expected least of all came like a thunder-bolt out of a clear sky. It happened one afternoon late in September just after the completion of the autumn round-up. Big Bill and Manito had gone away in the morning to look over the cattle in the very northern confines of the ranch close to the timber. There was some evidence that everything was not just as it should be with the herd.

At about five o'clock Manito came galloping back to the ranch house, riderless, and the saddle was splotched with blood. Hank Brodie ran out to catch him as he galloped into the ranch house yard and a minute later he was joined by Pony Perkins.

"My God in Heaven," exclaimed Pony, wringing his hands and turning as pale as it was possible for him to do under his sun-burned, wind-tanned skin, "my God, Bill told the truth. I couldn't believe it, I couldn't believe it."

"What's this nonsense you are talking," exclaimed Hank Brodie, sharply, "what do you mean?"

190

"I mean jest this, Hank, a terrible thing has come to us. Bill told me about it a-fore he rode away this morning. Pony, sez he, me and you has been good pals and I want to confide in you, Pony, I want to tell you something that I wouldn't tell anybody else in the world. I have a hunch I am going to get plugged today up in Aspen Draw. Don't laugh at me, Pony, but my father came to me this morning in a dream, you know he was a sky pilot, and he laid his hand on my head jest as he use'n to do when I was a kid. Willie, sez he, you're going to get plugged up in Aspen Draw today. It will be the rustlers that will do it. So make your peace with God.

"At first I thought Bill was joking, you know what a joker he was, but the more he talked the more I see he was in earnest and believed he was going to be plugged.

"Bill, sez I, if you think you are going to get plugged up there in Aspen Draw what makes you go there? Why don't you stay at home?

"Pony, sez he, there ain't no use kicking when the the time is set. The bullet that is going to get you will find you if you are fifty feet under ground. That's what old Bonaparte told one of his soldiers once. There ain't any use kicking against fate.

"I allowed Bill must be mistaken, I didn't see how it could be true, but he told me all that and more. He said as how he wanted us gents to bury him under the old cottonwood on the hilltop yonder. He said it was cool there in summer and sheltered in winter and there was lots of wild flowers. He said as how he didn't want any sky pilot from Wyanne or any other place shouting over his remains. He jes wanted me to say somethin' with you gents standin' around and then for us to lay him away jest like he had gone to sleep."

"Come, boys," said Hank, "let's saddle up. Pony, you and Larry come with me."

Two minutes later the three galloped out of the yard on their way to Aspen Draw. They found Big Bill just as his father had said, lying at the head of Aspen Draw. He was lying on his face just as he had pitched from Old Manito with a bullet hole in his head and his six gun lay beside him on the greensward and not a chamber was empty. There was evidence that he had come upon the rustlers unawares as they were driving a bunch of cattle into the timber. He had surprised them and they had shot him down like a dog.

The cow-punchers made a stretcher by cutting some fifteen foot poles and stretching a blanket on them. On this improvised hammock they laid Bill and carried him gently back to the ranch house. After he had been laid out in the bunk house, one of their number started for the nearest town to buy flowers. In his pocket he carried at least a month's wages for the entire ranch for every cow-puncher in the Crooked Creek outfit loved Old Bill. To some he was a chum and pal, to others he was a father, and to all he was a friend in times of need.

The following morning before sunup Pony, Long Tom, and Texas Jake started out to do some trailing. They returned about noon greatly excited. They had been successful beyond their fondest hopes. They had taken up the trail of the bunch of cattle that the rustlers had driven off and had followed it for five miles through very rough country, through many draws and canyons, to the headquarters of the rustlers.

That afternoon at about four o'clock the order was given for all the cow-punchers to saddle their horses and to look to their six guns.

"I am sorry, son," said Hank to his nephew, "but I am afraid you will have to come along to hold the horses. We want every man we've got for this enterprise."

"But what is the enterprise, Uncle Hank? What are you going to do?"

"We are going after those men and we are going to get them," returned his uncle.

"What will you do with them when you get them?" inquired Larry doubtfully.

"Well," said Hank, "that's more than I know. It will depend on how well I can control the boys, we may turn them over to the posse or it may turn out to be another necktie party."

"That has always seemed like a relic of barbarism," returned Larry. "I never could understand it. It doesn't seem just right."

"Well, son," explained his uncle, "it is this way. This state is young, only three or four years old, and our judicial systems are not well established. Many of our sheriffs are tenderfoots while all of the rustlers are gunmen and desperate characters. If we don't get them there is a chance they will get off scot free.

"Besides, the vigilance committee was the only judiciary this territory had before we became a state. It stood us in good stead then and it will now. For my part I can't see the difference between this and the judicial way of doing things in your eastern states. For instance, when the sheriff pulls the trigger that drops the murderer into eternity he is no more guilty of the murderer's death than is every citizen who votes for him."

"Well," said Larry, "if you look at it in that way perhaps there isn't so much difference."

It was a silent and determined little company of cowpunchers that rode away to get the men who had got their pal. There was very little talking among them and what there was, was carried on in low tones. As Larry looked from one to the other of his friends he was shocked by the stern look on the face of each. Their lips were set tight. In the eyes of each was a glint like steel. They certainly looked like men who had nerved themselves for a desperate enterprise.

After about two hours and a half of riding, just before sundown, they reached the point where Hank Brodie said they would leave their horses and go on foot. The bridle rein of each horse was attached to the one next him just as cavalry horses are held by one of their members when the rest go into battle. Only this time Larry held ten horses counting Patches.

As Hank Brodie and the little company filed away through the aisles of the forest, Larry looked after them with a strange tugging at his heart. Would they all be there when he next saw them? What would be the outcome of this desperate adventure? What a terrible life this frontier existence was when good citizens had to protect themselves against these rustlers with the might of their .45's. Hank had told Larry that it was a quarter of a mile to the rendezvous of the rustlers and it would take them at least half an hour to reach it. During this half hour Larry looked at his watch at least twenty times. Seconds were like minutes and minutes were like hours and as they dragged slowly by, Larry's nerves became keyed to a terrific pitch. He jumped with each snapping of a twig and the slightest sound set his heart to pounding. He was waiting and waiting and waiting for he knew not what.

Presently it came, a desultory shot from a .45 and then an agonized cry. Then more shots in quick succession like the setting off of a bunch of fire-crackers. Larry thought there must have been about thirty shots, then all was still, a strange unearthly silence. Even the trees and the bushes seemed to stand at attention waiting, waiting for they knew not what.

If the half hour until the encounter had been long, the next half hour was still longer. Who would be missing when they came in sight? What had been the outcome of the fight?

Presently he heard the sound of a footstep and his uncle appeared in sight.

"It's all right, son," shouted Hank Brodie, "don't worry, we are all here and not a man hurt."

Then his old friends, Long Tom, Pony Perkins, and Texas Jake and all the rest came filing into view. It was just as Hank Brodie had said, they were all there.

"How in the world did you all escape in such a fusillade as that?" asked Larry as soon as his uncle was in speaking range.

"Simple enough," returned the head cow-puncher. "We didn't have to fire a shot."

THE POSSE BEAT US TO IT BY ABOUT FIVE MINUTES

"What," exclaimed Larry in surprise, "you didn't fire a shot. Why, I heard at least thirty."

"Well, son, I am happy to inform you that they were not from our guns. The posse beat us to it by about five minutes. When we arrived on the scene they had gotten the entire rustler band. One was dead, and one was dying, though two will live to die on the gibbet."

The following afternoon six stalwart cow-punchers shouldered the casket which held the remains of their old pal, Bill, and marched up to the great cottonwood on the hilltop nearby. Then they set the casket upon the greensward close to the newly dug grave. No out-siders had been invited for this funeral, for, as Long Tom and Pony said, Bill would rather it would be just a home party without any fuss and feathers.

Finally after a long silence Pony rose and opened the Bible.

"Gents," he said, "I am going to read the twenty-third Psalm, but I want to explain to you cattle men, before I read it that this here David wan't no sech sheep man as we have today. He wan't no low-down miserable sort, but an honest-to-goodness, fair and square shepherd. I guess the cattle business hadn't got to going much in those days. Cattle ain't men-tioned much in the Bible.

" 'The Lord is my shepherd; I shall not want.' You

all know how careful we be in the springtime of the little new calves and colts, how we watch them and tend them and if they are sick we drive them to a sheltered spot and look after them.   Think what it would be, gents, to have the Lord for our shepherd.

" 'He maketh me to lie down in green pastures: He leadeth me beside the still waters.   He restoreth my soul.'   You folks all know how green the grass is on the upper mesa in June and you all remember how peaceful and clear the large pools are in Crooked Creek.   They are so transparent you can see the clouds in the heavens above reflected in their depths jest like they was a looking-glass.   It is jest that sort of grass, gents, and jest sech pools of water as them we will set beside on the heavenly range, 'cept it will be the water of the stream of life.   Don't you see, gents, how all that peaceful scene would restore your soul?

" 'He leadeth me in the paths of righteousness for His name's sake.'   We all know on this earthly way how easy it is to get in the paths of sin and what good traveling it is on the broad and smooth highway to perdition.   But up there the Lord hisself is goin' to keep our feet in the paths of righteousness, not because we are good ourselves, because we are all miserable sinners, but because He is good.

" 'Yea, though I walk through the valley of the shadow of death, I will fear no evil: for Thou art

with me; Thy rod and Thy staff they comfort me.'
Don't you remember, gents, away up in the big canyon
where the cliffs are three hundred feet high and straight
as a string, how dark it is and skeery? The sun shines
down there so little that there won't nothing grow,
but if you only knew the Lord was there, don't you
see how that would change things and a chap would
forget all about being lonesome? Well, that is the
way with the Lord when we go down in the valley
of the shadder, He is right there with us a-looking out
for us so we can't fear no evil because God is with
us. If we go to slip He reaches out his rod and
staff and holds us up.

" 'Thou preparest a table before me in the presence
of mine enemies: Thou anointest my head with oil; my
cup runneth over.' We all know how the Lord is
always preparing a table before us and how He makes
the bunch grass and the blue joint and pine grass
all grow for the cattle and how He gives us little calves
and colts in the spring and in the autumn, beef, and
how when we blows in at the ranch house after a
long day's work He anoints our heads with the oil
of gladness and He fills our cup of joy so full that
if we ain't careful we spill it.

" 'Surely goodness and mercy shall follow me all
the days of my life: and I will dwell in the house of
the Lord for ever.' Can't you see how on the heavenly

range everything is beautiful with goodness and mercy about us all the time and the Lord there a-looking on, what a glorious thing it will be for us to dwell in his great corral forever?"

Then to the accompaniment of a cabinet organ that had been moved up under the old cottonwood and which was played by Mrs. Morgan, wife of the manager, they sang that beautiful hymn, "Nearer my God to Thee." The hymn that has comforted wounded soldiers on the battle fields and dying men in hospital tents as well as the rich in their palatial chambers, a hymn which applies equally to rich and poor.

Nearer, my God, to Thee, Nearer to Thee;
E'en though it be a cross That raiseth me,
Still all my song shall be—Nearer, my God, to Thee!
Nearer, my God, to Thee! Nearer to Thee!

There let the way appear, Steps unto heaven;
All that Thou sendest me, In mercy giv'n;
Angels to beckon me, Nearer, my God to Thee!
Nearer, my God, to Thee! Nearer to Thee!

Or if, on joyful wing, Cleaving the sky,
Sun, moon, and stars forgot, Upward I fly,
Still all my song shall be—Nearer, my God, to Thee!
Nearer, my God, to Thee! Nearer to Thee!
Nearer, my God, to Thee! Nearer to Thee!

As the last beautiful line died away the cow-punchers noticed a heavy step on the greensward close at hand, and looking up, to their unspeakable amazement they beheld old Manito, Big Bill's faithful horse. How he had got out of the corral and what strange instinct had drawn him to the big cottonwood were equally inexplicable. But there he stood close to his master's casket looking down with a wistful gaze at the face of his master under the glass.

As Pony glanced over at the faithful horse, a great lump filled his throat.

"For heaven's sake, somebody take him away," choked Pony, "I can't preach with him standing there."

There was a long silence but no one started to do Pony's bidding. Finally Long Tom spoke up and everyone echoed in his heart the cow-puncher's sentiments.

"Pony," he said, "I guess he has the best right of anybody here. You jest draw in your belt and take a grip on yourself and go ahead."

So with a great effort Pony proceeded with the services, bowing his head in prayer.

"Dear Heavenly Father," he began, "we all knows that we ain't fit to call You Father, sech sinners as we be, but somehow we expect you to make allowances for all our shortcomings and to call us Your sons.

We all loved old Bill and want to say jest a few words for him. We are all hoping and praying, Lord that You won't be too hard on Bill for You know that we are all miserable sinners. There ain't no hiding our hearts from Thee for any time You want, You can jest take off the civer of our lives and peek inside. But Bill was a good sort and we loved him and his heart was as big as a teakettle.

"He might be kind of rough sometimes because he was so big and strong, especially if he thought a fellow was doing him, but with children he was as gentle as a woman and he always reverenced women.

"He was so generous if a fellow was down on his luck he would stick his big hand down in his pocket and give him his last dollar. We all loved him, Lord, and we are hoping and praying that You got some peaceful place for him on the heavenly range where he'll have a good horse to ride and the easy steers to rope."

Then the little cabinet organ struck up the familiar cow-puncher hymn, Rounded Up In Glory,* and the Crooked Creek cow-punchers sang it just as Larry had heard them that first night in the ranch house so many months before:

I have been thinking today, as my thoughts began to stray,
Of your memory to me worth more than gold.

*From Cowboy Songs collected by John A. Lomax, Macmillan Company.

As I ride across the plain, mid the sunshine and the rain,
You'll be rounded up in glory bye and bye.

Chorus

You'll be rounded up in glory bye and bye,
You'll be rounded up in glory bye and bye,
When the milling time is o'er.
And you'll stampede no more,
When He rounds you up, within the Master's fold.

May we lift our voices high, to that sweet bye and bye,
And be known by the brand of the Lord;
For His property we are, and He'll know us from afar,
When He rounds us up in glory bye and bye.

Chorus

You'll be rounded up in glory bye and bye,
You'll be rounded up in glory bye and bye,
When the milling time is o'er.
And you'll stampede no more,
When He rounds you up, within the Master's fold.

Then very reverently they lowered the casket covered with roses bought with the hard-earned money of Bill's chums into its last resting place. As it slowly sank from sight old Manito reached down his nose and nickered softly, not the eager whinney with which he had always greeted his master, but a wistful, pleading sound as though he were calling to him to come back.

Then they filled in the grave and covered it over

as well as they could with the greensward and laid
a great pile of roses upon it, the cow-punchers' last
tribute to their comrade.

As they started back to the ranch house some one
suggested that they had better put Manito back in
the corral but Hank Brodie said, "Let him alone.
Perhaps he had rather stay up here."

The last thing Hank did before he retired that
night was to go outside to look for Manito. To his
surprise he saw the faithful horse still standing under
the broad-spreading cottonwood.

The following day he was still near the tree. No
one saw him eat grass or go to the creek for water,
instead he seemed to be looking for somebody or
listening for something. The third day he was still
keeping his vigil and the fourth and the fifth. The
evening of the sixth day as the cow-punchers lounged
before the ranch house talking of Old Bill, Hank
Brodie said, "I think I will take the Winchester and
walk up to the old cottonwood. This sight of Manito
watching and waiting for his master is too much for
me."

"It is a good idea," said Pony, "it is bad enough to
see a human breaking his heart for those he loves,
but to see a horse is still worse."

"Me, too," put in Long Tom, "go ahead, Hank."

A few minutes later Hank walked slowly toward

the big cottonwood with his Winchester. Manito was standing about fifty yards from the tree and as Hank approached he raised his head to look at him. Then Hank raised the rifle and the watching cow-punchers listened for the short sharp report which they knew was coming, but it did not come.

As soon as the rifle butt touched Hank's shoulder old Manito threw up his head and broke into a wild gallop. He went straight as an arrow for the cottonwood. As he neared it all expected he would veer to one side, but instead he lowered his head and struck the butt of the tree fairly in the middle.

Hank Brodie ran to the spot where the faithful horse lay upon his master's grave. He raised the rifle but it was not needed. He let the butt fall to the ground and stood holding the barrel while he looked down at the horse.

Pony, Long Tom, and Larry and the rest of the cow-punchers lost no time in reaching the tree where Hank stood above the fallen horse.

"Well, gents," he said, "I didn't have to shoot. He broke his neck when he struck the tree. Killed him as though he had been struck by a stroke of lightning."

"Well, gents," put in Long Tom, "it is a comfort to know he has gone after Bill. If Bill needs a hoss on this here heavenly range Pony was telling us about, old Manito will be that hoss."

CHAPTER XI

THE RODEO AT WYANNE

IN the winter of the year 1897 the leading men of the little cattle city of Wyanne dreamed a dream and beheld a vision and in this dream they saw a great three days pageant or festival which should tell in detail the story of ranch life in the great west, especially the story of cattle raising. It must not be imagined, however, that they dreamed this dream one week and staged this great show the next or even the next month. For it took weeks and months of planning and much arduous labor to perfect the first American rodeo.

As soon as this scheme had been definitely outlined a large staff of secretaries were set to work corresponding with the leading cattle raisers both east and west of the Rocky Mountains. Horsemen from far and near were finally interested while many of the richest cattle raisers both east and west of the Rockies entered into the project with enthusiasm. There was no limit to the distance from which visitors would be invited and invitations were sent out as far west as the Pacific coast, south to the Rio Grande and northward to the Canadian border.

The great show was finally set for the first week in August. This was a quiet time on the ranches, the hay on the home ranches had all been cut and stacked, and there is a little breathing spell before the autumn round-up in September. So the time was opportune for this great western drama of the cattle men.

The first obstacle that the good people of Wyanne had to overcome was the fact that they had no arena large enough for such an event. But eons before the white men ever came to this continent nature had prepared just the place for the great show. It was about a mile from the center of the city and was a natural amphitheater which was christened the oval. There was a natural intervale about the size of a polo ground, perhaps three hundred yards by two hundred. This was surrounded by steep bluffs on three sides. The first thing that the Wyanne people did was to build a half mile race track skirting the foot of the bluffs. This was then fenced inside and out by a five-foot board fence. The enclosure inside the inner fence was then levelled until it was as smooth as a billiard table. This arena contained between twenty-five or thirty acres.

Bleachers were then set up on the buffs on three sides of the track. The first seats were about ten feet above the track while those perched on the highest seat could view this beautiful arena from an elevation of nearly a hundred feet. Seats for twenty thousand people were made while as many more could be accommodated on the grass.

For several weeks before the great event small companies of people both in Wyanne and in the surrounding towns and cities were very busy. They were rehearsing for their parts, practising their stunts, and also making floats for the great parade which was to inaugurate the important day.

The first day of the rodeo was ushered in by as beautiful weather as could be wished for. The air was clear and not too hot, the mountains to the west of Wyanne were looking beautiful in their summer verdure.

The great parade formed on the main street of Wyanne with its many sections resting upon the side streets. Finally at one o'clock the herald and the leading band started and the machinery which was to set in motion the first American rodeo had begun to move. Immediately following the band were five hundred mounted cow-punchers upon some of the best horses that the west could produce, cow-punchers from Wyoming, South Dakota, Oregon, California, New Mexico and Arizona. They were gay in their cow-puncher regalia with the broad Stetsons, the bright kerchiefs, the ornate chaps, and the tall, shiny riding boots. The chains in the bits of their horses jingled merrily as they marched along.

They were closely followed by two hundred cow girls many of whom were society girls from the best families in the west, girls who had taken prizes at riding shows and races and whose greatest hobby in the world was horses. Some of these girls, however, were typical cow girls, born and brought up on the ranch, who had ridden horses ever since they were large enough to climb to a horse's back. A few of them were famous riders who had ridden some of the worst outlaws in the west.

The cow girls were followed by three hundred Indians gay in their war paint, war bonnets and bright blankets. These Indians were Sioux from the local reservation, Black Feet from the hills of Montana, Navahos from Arizona, and New Mexico, all riding beautiful horses with the ornate Mexican saddles. While still others were Apaches from a distant reservation, but all were as gay in color as the traditional red man.

These horsemen were followed by nearly fifty floats representing life in the great west. First there was the log cabin of the settler, a rude affair which merely sheltered him from the wind and the rain. There was the camp of the Indian, his teepee on the edge of the forest.

These were followed by the old stage coach and
the ox-cart, also a canoe, all upon wheels and looking
as natural as life.   The plow and the reaper were
also shown.   Then came a dozen floats representing
the industries of the state, the mining camp, the oil
well, the sheep ranch and many others.   Then the
fraternities of Wyanne and other local towns took
their turn upon the floats.   After these came several
marching columns representing different industries and
fraternities of the city of Wyanne and other towns
of the cattle land.   And all this vast parade which
extended for nearly two miles was interspersed with a
dozen bands which blared their triumphal music as
the procession moved on.   It was just two o'clock
when the end of the procession passed the reviewing
stand at the oval.   Then the cowboys and the cow girls
put their horses which were to take part in the day's
sport in the paddock which had been provided for
them and the great crowd which had both preceded
and followed the procession finally seated itself in
the half circle of seats which surrounded the track
on three sides.

Four bands were stationed at different points around
the track to amuse the crowd and to keep it good-
natured until the first event should occur.   On three
sides of the track, perched high in great trees which
had been spared for this special purpose, were three

men. Each was equipped with a megaphone, a pair
of strong lungs and a stentorian voice. Previous to
each event these three men lifted their megaphones and
sent the announcements ringing across the intervale to
the twenty-five thousand spectators seated on the bluffs.

The first event, in honor to the ladies, was the cow
girls' mile and a half relay race. Each cow girl was
allowed three horses, usually her own string, and two
helpers. It was a half mile track and when a contestant came sweeping around to the finish of the
first half mile on her madly racing pony, she had to
bring him to a dead stop, changing the saddle and
bridle to another horse which her first helper was
holding and then when everything was in readiness,
they were off again. The lightning cinch was most
valuable in this race, merely a sharp pull and a twist
of the wrist and the trick was done. It was incredible
how quick these expert horse-women could change
the saddles and bridles on their steeds. When they
came around the second time there was still another
pony and another lightning change and they were off
for the final lap. If a buckle stuck or there was any
trouble in making the change the race was lost. It
was quite as much a race of dexterity of change as
it was a race of good horses.

The second event was even more spectacular and
thrilling than the first for it was nothing more or

less than a race between four old-fashioned stage
coaches. The coaches were furnished by the manage-
ment. They were standing at the scratch, while the
six horses which were used on each were in the paddock near at hand. Each driver was allowed as many
helpers as he cared to employ. At the sound of the
gong there was a great scrambling in the paddock
for the horses. They came forth almost at a gallop
and in an incredibly short time they were harnessed
to the coach and the driver was perched upon his
high seat, the reins in his left hand and the long
snake-like whip in his right. Then the whip cracked
and the six excited horses sprang into the collars and
they were off. The coaches swayed and the axles
snapped as they got up speed. The gait of the horses
was a head-long gallop and each horse was trying to
outdo the rest of the team. This was a race which
required the greatest skill by the driver and the keenest
judgment in calculating the turns as there was much
jockeying for positions. The race was for two miles
so the old stage coaches rattled four times around the
track while the crowd cheered as their favorite drew
to the front.

The excitement while the race lasted was intense,
nearly every one in the grand stand was standing on
his feet and shouting, when the leading coach finally
thundered down the home stretch and claimed the

prize money, which was enough to buy six horses and a brand new coach.

Thinking that the crowd had had excitement enough for the present, the next feature was more sober. It was the great mounted cavalcade of cowboys and cow girls. The five hundred cowboys and the two hundred cow girls who had come out in the parade half an hour before again mounted their steeds and rode slowly around the track. As they passed the judges' stand they were carefully inspected and the most typical cowboy and cow girl each received a handsome purse of gold.

The fourth event was also historic for it was nothing more or less than a relay pony express race, a race intended to show the efficiency of the pony express and what it had meant to the west as a means of communication.

Each contestant was allowed two horses and two assistants. The distance for the race was one mile, the first horse was to run the first quarter and the third quarter, the second horse the second and the fourth.

When a madly racing express pony reached the end of the first quarter his rider had to dismount, then put the saddle and bridle on the new horse who was standing nearby and also to change his mail bags. When everything was in readiness he was off again.

At the end of the second quarter he found his first pony waiting for him and once more the saddle and bridle and the mail bags had to be shifted. At the end of the third quarter the second pony was again waiting and the shift was again made. So it will be seen that this race was also a race of dexterity in shifting the trappings of the horses as well as a race testing the speed of the ponies. A slip with the bridle or saddle, or the mail sacks and the race was lost.

The cow girl bucking contest was also a spectacular event and awaited with eager interest because of the fact that the contestants were women. The horses that they rode were not the outlaws that the men rode in their contest, instead they were what are called show buckers, horses that had been trained and encouraged to buck, horses that enjoyed bucking and took it as a sort of game. They never tried to kill their riders, but they did try to dismount them and these cow girls stuck to their saddles like leeches. Crowhopping, sunfishing, straight bucking, and swapping ends were nothing to them, even when a horse stood on his hind legs they did not mind, provided he did not try the back throw. These maneuvers were so tremendous that the average horse-women gasped with fear just to watch them and they breathed a sigh of relief when the contest was over.

The pony race for the Indians was in lighter vein and intended partly for fun. The Indians rode without saddles guiding their horses merely with halters, and clad only in their war bonnets and breech cloths. The ponies that they rode were of all sorts and sizes and the race always created much amusement although the Indians rode with great ease and skill.

The steer roping contest was eagerly watched by the thousands of cow-punchers and cattle men. This event was staged on the arena inside the track. The steer was driven in through a gateway in the board fence and allowed a thirty foot start of the cow-puncher who was mounted on his favorite pony. The steer was a dogie, the long horn Texas variety, as wild as an antelope. As soon as the cow-puncher came within roping distance, his lariat shot out. If it fell true it would catch the steer over the horns. At a sign from his rider the cow-pony stiffened his legs like pile drivers and braced to meet the shock of a thousand pounds of madly galloping steer. As the lariat came taut the steer usually reared into the air three or four feet and, if the rope or cinch didn't break, he landed heavily upon his side. Then the clever cow-pony held the rope taut while his master jumped to the ground and with two or three passes of a rope hog-tied the steer. All this had to be done inside two minutes and the quickest time took first money.

Bull-dogging steers was a kindred event and that was also staged on the glass plot.   As in the case of roping, the steer was driven in and allowed a thirty foot start. The cow-puncher mounted upon his favorite pony went after the steer like the wind and at just the right moment sprang from the saddle and threw his right arm over the neck of the madly galloping steer.   Then with each hand he seized a horn and with a sharp pull of his left hand brought the steer's head around and threw him heavily upon his right side.   He had to be thrown with all four legs stretched out and with his head laid down flat on the ground. The cow-puncher had to hold him with one hand while he waved his other hand to the judges.

The cowboys' bucking contest was one of the great events of the rodeo.   For this occasion the country for hundred of miles around had been scoured for outlaw horses.   Some of them even rated as killers. The conditions were very hard, a cow-puncher was allowed an assistant to help saddle the horse. He was not allowed a bridle but had to guide the horse with a halter.   He had to ride sitting erect, he couldn't pull leather, that is catch hold of the saddle to save himself from a bad fall and each time the horse bucked he had to wave his hat to the audience.   Al-

THE BLACK FURY REARED UPON HIS HIND LEGS

together it was a very spectacular performance and one which required supreme horsemanship.

For the first and second days of the rodeo in each contest the winning horse was held and passed up to the finals for the third day and the rest were eliminated from the contest. So those who survived for this supreme effort were in what was called the world's championship class.

The third day of the Wyoming rodeo dawned as auspicious as the other two had and by half past twelve every seat in the vast arena had been taken and ten thousand were sitting on the grass. The contests for that day were many and the sports were to begin at one o'clock. We will pass over most of the events and come at once to the cowboy's bucking contest. For this occasion an outlaw horse with the fearful reputation as a killer had been reserved. He was a stallion called Big Thunder.

The first cow-puncher who undertook to ride him lasted about ten seconds. After several high bucks and the sunfishing maneuver, and then a combination of bucking and sunfishing which was all his own, Big Thunder sent his rider sprawling in the dust and he was out of the contest.

The second cowboy fared no better for after three high straight-away bucks of terrific proportions blood spurted from the man's nostrils and he clung to the saddle and so was disqualified.

The third man lasted through all the preliminary bucking and sunfishing, but when Big Thunder attempted the back throw he was obliged to drop from the saddle to the ground to save his life.

The fourth man lasted for twenty seconds and then dropped the halter rope and the black fury bolted for the board fence that skirted the track. He went over it like a deer and started for the distant paddock. The cow-punchers were barely able to stop him and because he had lost control of the horse by dropping the rope he was disqualified.

Because of the fact that Big Thunder had spilled four of the best cow-punchers east of the Rockies there was only one more left and this was a lank Californian who fared no better than his predecessors. After a series of maneuvers which combined everything that the black fury had done to the other four contestants the Californian was dismounted and Big Thunder was still unridable.

At this stage in the performance the announcers from the crow-nests on the three sides of the track gave out an announcement calling for a volunteer to ride the black fury.

"What, gentlemen," cried the announcers, "will you let this horse beat you? Is there no one in all this vast audience who dares to ride Big Thunder?"

For a moment no one seemed forthcoming, then a tall, slim young man sprang to his feet and cried, "I will ride him, gentlemen, I will ride Big Thunder."

At the sound of his nephew's voice, Hank Brodie sprang to his feet. "Gentlemen," he called, " I forbid it.   He is a minor and I am his guardian.   He is booked for the great two-mile race which follows this contest and I forbid him to ride Big Thunder."

At this point two strong hands reached up and pulled Hank Brodie down.   His two friends, Pony Perkins and Long Tom, had taken him in charge.

"Don't spoil the boy's fun," pleaded Long Tom, "I bet you he can ride him. He is a wonderful rider and he has a great way with horses."

"I will bet on him, too," put in Pony. "I will bet the Jack Rabbit he can ride the black devil."

"What is your decision, Mr. Brodie, will he ride?" cried one of the judges and Hank nodded his head.

Whether Big Thunder had worked off a lot of his steam and pure cussedness was not known but it was certain that Larry fared much better than had any of the others.   He mounted with a quick spring and caught the halter rope with a strong sure hand. The black fury executed his three long high jumps which had put the second contestant out of business, but at each jump Larry raised slightly in the saddle and took a part of the blow on the stirrups and so saved himself. Sunfishing and swapping ends did not discomfort him, but Hank Brodie felt his heart in his throat when the black fury reared upon his hind legs for the back throw.

"By God, he is going over," exclaimed the head cowpuncher of the Crooked Creek ranch, "the boy will be killed."

But the black stallion did not lose his balance, instead he cavorted about upon his hind legs for a few seconds and then came down with a vicious slap of his fore feet upon the ground.   Then the deviltry seemed to go out of him and instead of going through the fence as the crowd expected he went straight around the race track at a terrific gallop, just the thing Larry wanted him to do. The second time he came around Larry was able to pull him down before the judges' stand and make him stand quietly, entirely subdued for the first time during the contest.

As Larry waved his hat to the judges, the thirty thousand people in the amphitheater rose to their feet as of one accord and gave vent to their enthusiasm in a mighty chorus of cheers, cheers that even drowned the utmost efforts of the four bands which sought to swell the bedlam.   It was a great triumph for the young man but sweetest of all his praise was that from Long Tom and Pony when they came down from their seats and shook him warmly by the hand.

"We knowed you could do it," said Long Tom. "We

was betting on you. It was us that made your Uncle Henry let you ride."

"That first night when you came to the ranch," said Pony, "you said as how your riding master reckoned you could ride any kind of horse that lived. We cow-punchers sort of snickered in our sleeves that night, but today the joke is on us and we all have to admit you can do it."

CHAPTER XII

THUNDERING HOOFS

PROBABLY the most thrilling event for the entire three days was the great free-for-all two-mile running race which was next staged. Every one had been talking about it since the first day of the rodeo and, if the truth is told, probably many bets had been placed. The race was supposed to bring together some of the finest running horses to be found anywhere west of the Mississippi River, between the Rio Grande and the Canadian line. When the seven starters finally lined up under the wire beside the judges' stand they represented all types of running horses. To the astonishment of all, Pony Perkins on his mouse-colored Jack Rabbit was there. Pony had won a half mile race the day before with the Jack Rabbit and this success had gone to his head. Against the better judgment of Hank Brodie and Long Tom and the rest of the Crooked Creek cow-punchers he had entered the little horse for this long hard race. His friends had expostulated with him in vain and there he was at the pole.

"Well," said Long Tom to Hank Brodie as Pony had hurried away to the paddock fifteen minutes before, "he is a sensible chap about most everything in this world but he goes fairly nutty about that little hoss of his. Why, the Jack Rabbit may last for half a mile, but after that he won't even be a spectator."

Next to the Jack Rabbit stood our old friend Patches called for this race, Prince Patches. He was ridden by his beloved master, Larry Winton. The two horses contrasted strangely. The Jack Rabbit was the typical mouse-colored mustang with large ears, an ewe neck, thin mane and tail, and rather insignificant to look at. But for a short dash he was really a very fast horse. Patches, on the other hand, although he was part mustang, looked every inch of him the thoroughbred. He was a bright bay with three cream-colored spots on one side and four on the other. His ears were small, his head was clean-cut, his eyes were full of fire and his nose was as soft as velvet, his crest was beautifully arched, his mane and tail were heavy and his shoulders and flanks were muscular and powerful. His legs were clean-cut and he stood well upon his toes like a thoroughbred.

Next to him stood a black stallion called Arizona Knight. He was from the great stock farm near Tucson, a horse of Mexican breeding and probably of Moorish origin. He was said to be the fastest horse in the southwest.

Next to him stood Knocka-knees, a milk-white mus-

tang from the great Sioux reservation. He was ridden
by an Indian boy and said to be the fastest horse owned
by the Sioux nation. He had some of the mustang
characteristics although he showed breeding as well.

Next to the white favorite of the Sioux came King
California, called King Cal, a large gray running
horse from the great stock farm at Palo Alto. He was
tall and rangy with little excess fat and he looked like
a great runner. Next to him was the Antelope, a tall
roan, the pride of the Black Feet Indians. He also
was ridden by an Indian boy. The last in line was
Rainbow, a splendid chestnut gelding of English origin
perhaps descended from a bard, from a horse ranch in
southeastern Montana. Rainbow, King Cal and Arizona Knight had all taken prizes in running races and
were rated as three of the best horses in the west.

Larry had received hasty instructions from his uncle
before taking his place in the race.

"Now remember, boy," Uncle Henry had said, "that
this two-mile race is a regular marathon for horses. A
half-mile horse like the Jack Rabbit is of no earthly use.
Even a good mile and one-eighth running horse could-
n't stand the racket. This race would kill some of
the best mile and one-quarter running horses. It is the
last long mile that counts. Don't forget that, but save
your horse during the first mile. You just try to keep
him fresh. Let the rest of them spurt and you trail.

Remember it is the last mile that counts, even then do
not shove him for all he is worth until the last quarter.
It is the finish that tells.   Good luck, boy, we are all
betting on you."

As everybody had expected at the crack of the pistol
the Jack Rabbit sprung into the lead.   Pony saw to
that, even if he could not be in at the end of the race
he was going to have some glory for his little horse so
he didn't spare the small mustang, but put him at once
to his best pace.   The Indian boy on Knocka-knees
also had this intention and he and Pony had a lively
race up to the half, but Pony and the Jack Rabbit led
at the half by a hundred feet.   They were closely followed by the Antelope who could better afford an early
spurt than they could for he had wind like a moose.
The rest of the horses were contented to trail on behind
these racers who had set out to cover the first half mile
in record-breaking time.

At the half as everyone had expected the Jack Rabbit began to show signs of slackening.   Knocka-knees
and the Antelope passed him and by the three-quarters
he was at the tail end of the procession nearly a hundred feet behind.

At the three-quarters Knocka-knees and the Antelope staged a brilliant run to the finish of the first mile
and they came in under the wire fifty yards ahead of the
rest of the horses.   Larry did not mind that he and

Patches were at the tail end of this procession for he was remembering what his uncle had said and was saving his horse.

As Patches passed under the wire at the end of the first mile, however, a new spirit seemed to animate him. For there was born in his heart and brain a new idea. It was not his own but was an inheritance; it came to him through generations of racing ancestors. It was the heritage of his great-grandfather who had broken the world's record at Churchill Downs, and it even ante-dated that for it was the soul of his Arabian forbears, horses fleet as the wind, who had carried Arabian shieks over the desert in record-breaking time. It was this heritage that came surging into Patches' veins causing his heart beat to quicken and his muscles and sinews to receive new life. In this race, at the very second that he passed under the wires at the end of the first mile, Prince Patches, the American race horse was born.

With the beginning of the second mile Larry began feeling out his horse by shoving him forward. His uncle had shouted to him as he passed the grand stand. He had not made out what he said amid the cheers of the crowd but he knew it was an admonishment to settle down to business and to begin the long hard fight ahead.

At the end of the eighth Larry found himself seem-

ingly in a pocket behind Knocka-knees and the Antelope with the three other horses perhaps fifty feet ahead.
He tried first the pole and then the outside, but each
time he moved over to pass, the horse ahead of him
moved to check his progress. Three times they did this
and then the game was apparent to Larry. These two
horses were trying to put him out of the race. At the
thought great indignation welled up in the boy's heart
and he eagerly watched for an opportunity to outwit
the strategy. Presently it came, Knocka-knees surged
over a yard or so away from the Antelope and at that
instant Larry let the quirt fall heavily on Patches' side
and called to him in a ringing voice. No one of the
thirty thousand excited spectators, or even the judges
in the grand stand, ever knew just how it was done.
Some said Patches went through the opening like an
express train, others said he went like a bullet and you
could not see him at all. But when he had passed, the
beautiful Knocka-knees limped into the ditch with a
dislocated stifle and his part in the race was done. The
Antelope, too, had been so much upset by the jar that
Patches had given him as he passed that he lost his
stride and when he finally regained it he was two
lengths behind, but he was a great running horse and
the Indian boy who rode him was a cunning driver
and at the end of an eighth of a mile he had drawn up
abreast of Patches. They held these relative positions,

FOOT BY FOOT PATCHES DREW AHEAD OF HIS ADVERSARIES

Rainbow, King Cal and Arizona Knight in the lead and Patches and the Antelope fifty feet behind them, up to the three-eighths mark. Even at the half the position was relatively the same, only Patches and the Antelope had moved up to within twenty-five feet of the other horses. Then it was that Larry steeled his will and brought his quirt into play. They were now going like the wind. The air cut Larry's face like a March breeze. The continual roll of hoof beats was in his ears. The track ahead of him was a brown blur and the mighty audience on his right was a backward rushing mass.

At the five-eighths mark the five horses were running neck and neck, but the Antelope had clearly been pushed to his limit and was wavering and before the three-quarters was reached he began to fall behind. Patches on the other hand began to show his mettle. Foot by foot, yard by yard, he crept up on the other three horses until at the three-quarters the four matchless racers were running neck to neck. Then King Cal's rider lashed him mercilessly with the quirt and by sheer force drove him two lengths ahead until half of the next eighth had been covered. Then he collapsed and fell behind and Patches moved up to take his place. Next Rainbow was shoved to the end of his endurance and he, too, forged ahead for a length, but at the seven-eighths fell behind and left the race for Patches and Arizona Knight.

The finishing line was just forty rods away. Up to this point Larry had used his quirt the least of any of the drivers and even now he felt that he could do more with Patches through love than he could with the whip. So he leaned over and patted him on the neck and talked to him. "Patches," he said, "Go, go, your master wants you to go. Heigh, heigh, go." If Patches had responded magnificently beneath the quirt, beneath the caress of his master's voice he became dynamic. Larry felt the great muscles in his shoulders and hips intensify. He felt the mighty effort that this splendid racing machine was making just as plainly as though he had been the horse himself, and in fact horse and rider were one and that is why Patches knew what his master wanted. Seeing that his voice availed him more than the quirt he dropped the whip by his side and continued to talk to Patches, "Go, heigh, go." Foot by foot Patches drew ahead of his adversaries. At first it was barely perceptible, just a nose length, then half a neck, then a full neck, and at the end of the two miles he thundered under the wire half a length ahead of the black racing horse from Arizona and the race was won. As Larry brought his beloved steed to a standstill two hundred feet beyond the judges' stand he appreciated what a terrible strain the race had been. In spite of all he could do his senses reeled and he clung to the horn of his saddle while the mighty cheering of the crowd about him became indistinct and incoherent. But this only lasted for a second or two, then his fine vitality asserted itself and he pulled himself together. Yes, it was true, this mighty crowd of thirty thousand men and women were shouting it. Prince Patches had won, and this made him the greatest running horse west of the Mississippi River and one of the greatest in the entire world.

Then as a sort of grand finale to the great race which had seemingly stretched the nerves of the excited crowd to the breaking point, there was enacted as a sort of anti-climax a feature known as the wild horse race.

Fifteen or twenty wild horses from the plains had been secured for this event. So far as was known these horses had never had a bridle or saddle upon them. They were like other wild animals, keenly suspicious of man and ready to fight for their freedom and their lives to the last ounce of their strength. One by one these wild horses were delivered to the contesting cow-punchers on the arena inside the inner fence. One of the cow-punchers was mounted upon his favorite pony with rope in readiness and was allowed several helpers. His stunt was to rope and throw the wild horse and then to blindfold, saddle and bridle him and ride him once around the track. It was a sort of impromptu wild horse breaking done under the watch. If a cow-puncher failed to subdue his steed in a certain number

of minutes he was disqualified and some one else took
his place.

Then for the next hour and a half the audience beheld the most hair-raising incidents that they had yet
seen during the rodeo.　There were broncs upon four
legs and broncs upon two legs, cow-punchers in the
saddle and cow-punchers flying through the air or
sprawling in the dirt.　Some of the latter limped away
with sprained ankles or nursed sprained wrists while
one poor fellow had to be carried away on a stretcher
and it was subsequently learned that he had ridden his
last race.

These practically wild horses squealed, snorted, and
bucked, kicked, and bit, and the cow-puncher had to
act like lightning, always keeping his head.　Occasionally a woman shrieked or covered her eyes or even
fainted, men who were enured to such scenes gasped
in fear and astonishment.　Several horses crashed
through the inner fence and before the contest was over
much of this fence was in kindling wood.　One of the
frantic broncs finally leaped the outside fence and before the audience was aware of what was happening
was in among the spectators, but men had been placed
in readiness for such an event and the frantic horse
was almost immediately enmeshed in half a dozen lari-
ats and rendered helpless.

When the great audience had shouted, screamed,

laughed, and wept until every man, woman and child in the concourse was nearly a physical wreck the last cow-puncher rode the last wild horse to the paddock and the rodeo was over. Then to the music of the bands the oval was emptied and this great western assembly from half a dozen states representing all walks of life made their way back to Wyanne and thence to their homes. They had seen the first of the American rodeos and felt well repaid with the entertainment. They did not know it then but they had seen a feature of western entertainment which was destined to become historic and the little cattle city of Wyanne had led the way.

CHAPTER XIII

RACING AGAINST DEATH

IT was not until the third year of their life together upon the Crooked Creek ranch that the friendship and understanding between Patches and Larry ripened into its greatest perfection. Up to this time they had been the best of pals, doing the day's work together like good chums. The understanding between them even thus far had been remarked by the rest of the cow-punchers on the ranch, but with the beginning of the third year Patches evinced an understanding of his master and anticipated his wishes in a way that quite amazed the other cow-punchers.

The first indication of Patches' uncommon understanding came late in March, when Larry was taken ill, first with a hard cold and then with an attack of bronchitis. Larry and Patches had been doing most of the range riding that winter. For two or three weeks they had been searching for sick cows and calves. It was the season of the year when the strength of the herd was at its lowest ebb, and the stock had sometimes gone for days when the snow was deepest with very little food. The cows with new calves were often taken with pneumonia, while the calves frequently became so chilled during the first two or three days that they never got over it. It was the range rider's work to look up these animals and drive them to places of shelter and see that they had food.

One morning about the twentieth of March when Larry did not come to the corral as usual, Patches was rather surprised and watched for him for two or three hours, then finally gave up and settled down to the dullness of a day in the corral. But when the same thing happened the following morning he was still more surprised. He greeted each one of the cow-punchers when they came into the corral with a friendly nicker and when he discovered it was not his master his disappointment was very apparent. Two days was bad enough, but when this thing had gone on for five days, Patches became quite desperate and tried several times to slip by such old friends as Pony and Long Tom when they came into the corral. But seeing his efforts frustrated, on the fifth morning he took matters into his own hands.

Larry was resting comfortably in the bunk house. He was not very ill but the doctor had said that he must remain in bed for several days, resting and recuperating his strength. It was about nine o'clock in the morning and Larry had fallen into a pleasant morning doze, when he was awakened by a terrific bang in the hallway leading to the bunk house proper. It sounded to him as though a portion of the great front door had toppled over on the floor. Then he heard the sound of heavy steps in the hallway. He was greatly surprised and, wrapping a blanket over his shoulders and slipping on his shoes, hastened to the door leading to the hallway. As he opened it his astonishment may well be imagined when the beautiful head of Patches was thrust through the doorway into his face.

"Good gracious! Where in thunder did you come from, pal? What are you doing here in the bunk house? I'll have to get you out or you will go through the floor."

Larry hastily shut the door and putting on more clothes entered the hallway and very carefully backed Patches out of the front door, then he called for help. Pony soon came running in answer to his hellos and Patches was taken away and hitched in a stable to his great disgust. Only once or twice before in his whole life had he ever been tied up in one of these niggardly box stalls. As soon as Larry was well enough to have visitors, Pony would bring Patches around to the window by the head of his master's bed and they would hold a short confab through the open widow. Larry would smooth and pat Patches' head and talked to him until he had satisfied the craving of the fine animal for his master's company for that day.

It was a joyous morning when Larry and Patches were again riding over the range at their accustomed work. Then it was that Larry noticed that Patches had seemingly developed a strange perspicacity and knowledge of his own thought. They would be poking along some trail going at a slow walk when the thought would come to Larry that he ought to be hurrying up. Patches would anticipate his master's wishes and break into the habitual running trot. Or some evening just before sunset they would be riding a distant portion of the ranch and Larry would conclude that he had done enough for that day and think to himself that it was about time to quit. Usually before he had entertained these thoughts for many seconds Patches would turn about and make a bee line for the ranch house.

This perspicacity of the horse was also most effective during the round-up season. If Larry singled out a steer away at the center of a large bunch of several hundred cattle, he had only to fix his mind steadfastly upon that particular animal and Patches would raise his head and look over the seething herd until he had spotted the animal in question, then he would start pushing this way and that until he had found the coveted steer, after which he would drive him out into the open in the shortest possible time.

One morning in early July, Patches and Larry had an adventure which the young man never forgot. In fact, it was burned so deeply into his memory that for weeks afterward he would occasionally spring up in bed during sleep and cry out, thinking that once again he was at the heart of the terrible maelstrom that had so nearly overwhelmed him.

It was a beautiful July morning, the American birthday in fact, but it was more like a June day than a July day. The sky was of that dreamy far-away blue which suggests infinite distance. Great white clouds were floating across the blue like stately ships. The distant mountains looked more like a range from dreamland than real peaks and cliffs of interchanging rock and forest. The air was soft and balmy, sparrows were chipping in the grass, Piñon birds were scolding in the thickets, and a sense of infinite peace was over all the land. It was one of those days which make a man gaze, first at the blue sky, then at the distant mountains, then at the green pasture land close at hand, and finally, when he had drunk in all this ravishing beauty, to heave a deep sigh, stretch his muscles and thank God for life. This was just what Larry did and then he noticed that he and Patches had stopped upon a sunny slope of the mesa where wild strawberries were plenty, so he dismounted and allowed the horse to graze upon the green grass while he ate wild strawberries much as he had done when he was a lad in that far away New England.

He was so interested in his search for the strawberries and they were so delicious that he wandered many rods from the spot where he had dismounted, in fact he passed over the top of the nearest ridge and part way down the slope beyond. Then he saw on the slope opposite fifty or seventy-five cattle feeding, with still more on the top of the opposite ridge. He did not, at first, think very much about it but stood looking at them. Nearly all of them had their heads down feeding while some were standing in ruminative attitudes looking off, like himself, across the landscape.

There were a dozen little calves in the herd and they were frisking about enjoying the warm summer sunlight and their own freedom upon the great plateau.

Then one of the cows nearest Larry raised her head and looked squarely at him and as though by some psychological action on the rest of the herd another head bobbed up and this cow also gazed straight at the man who was perhaps a hundred yards away on the opposite slope. Then other heads were raised until presently forty or fifty of the cattle which had been feeding a minute before were looking at the solitary man on the nearby hillside. Then the cow which had first noticed Larry began slowly walking toward him and another followed, and another, and another until twenty or thirty of the herd were in motion. But before they had covered fifty feet the walk changed into

a slow trot and that in turn to a quick gallop and almost
before Larry appreciated the sinister thing that was
sweeping down upon him the entire herd had broken
into a mad gallop.

Then Larry remembered something that Hank
Brodie had told him the first day he had ridden with
his uncle on the Crooked Creek ranch. His uncle had
said a herd of cattle is like the sea, the sea can smooth
out all its little ripples until it looks like the most peaceful thing in the world, but in a few minutes it can
break into mighty billows scattering death and destruction in their wake. So it is with a herd of cattle, the
first law of the cattle land is never dismount in sight
of the herd and never be caught off your horse if
you value your life.

Larry's first thought was of Patches, he was only a
few rods away and he turned and ran with all his might
towards the spot where he had left his faithful horse,
but to his great surprise as he topped the crest and
looked down the further slope Patches was not there.
What did it mean? He surely had left him just over
the swell. Then he looked back at the herd of cattle.
They were coming on, heads down and tails up, at a
terrific pace. The thunder of their hoofs could be
heard like the rolling of many great drums. It was a
sinister sight, so he bent his every energy and ran as
he had not run in many a day. Surely Patches was

just over the top of the next crest. He had been mistaken in the position where he had left him. The truth was that Larry in his great haste had gone in the wrong direction and instead of going towards his horse was going away from him in an oblique direction.

Although he ran with all his might, yet when he reached the top of the swell the herd topped the crest where he had been a minute before. So he put forth still greater effort and reached the top of the next crest and saw to his utter consternation that Patches was nowhere in sight. Then a great fear clutched him. He was helpless here upon the open plain with no tree or huge rock to shelter him, and no horse upon whose back he might climb to escape the terrible thing that was sweeping down upon him. He ran with all his remaining strength, he ran until his breath came in wheezy gasps, yet do the best he could, as he topped the next crest the herd came sweeping up the slope behind him only fifty yards away. Then it was that Larry thought he heard other hoofs from another direction. Another herd must be sweeping down upon him, his plight was even more desperate than he had imagined, but as he turned his head to see how close this new danger was, he saw to his great surprise two horses sweeping down upon him like the wind. One was Old Baldy and his uncle was upon his back and the other was Patches. Uncle Henry was holding Patches by the bridle rein with his left hand while he applied his quirt to both horses and they were running at a headlong gallop. Larry saw at once that his uncle was planning to meet the oncoming cattle at an angle of forty-five degrees and was curving in just as close to the herd as he dared to and his thought was that at just the right moment Patches would sweep up to the frantically running cattle and then Larry could mount while they were still going at a gallop. It was a desperate chance, a slip of the foot or hand and all would be over, but it was the only chance they had so Larry put forth the last remaining ounce of strength in his strong muscles as the galloping horses swept down almost in the face of the charging herd. Then it was that Larry's feat of mounting while Patches was going at a gallop, which he had practised so faithfully two years before stood him in good stead, for as the horses swept by so close to the herd that before they could turn both Patches and Baldy were struck by the horns of the frantic cattle, Larry clutched the horn of his saddle and with all his remaining strength threw himself across the haven of Patches' back. It was but the work of an instant to gain the saddle and with a sharp pull on the right rein both Baldy and Patches surged to the right and became a part of the madly rushing herd. In this way they not only saved their riders but they saved themselves from the terrible stampede.

THE HERD CAME SWEEPING UP THE SLOPE BEHIND HIM

They had gone only fifty yards further when the cattle of their own accord began to slow down. The surprise and consternation upon the individual members of the herd was plainly noticeable. They did not in the least associate Larry on horseback with the fleeing man on foot. They had seen that figure so often they thought him a part of the horse.

Seeing how pale his nephew was and how nervous, Hank Brodie rode by his side with one hand on his shoulder until they were safely out of the milling herd.

"Thank God," exclaimed Uncle Henry fervently, when they were at last out of danger. "You see I heard the sound of stampeding hoofs and discovered Patches just in time. Two seconds later, boy, and there wouldn't have been enough of you left for a respectable funeral. It was a marvelous escape and should teach you a lesson you will never forget."

Another desperate race with death Larry and Patches had during that third eventful year upon the ranch, but this second race was quite different from the first. In the first instance they had raced to save their own lives, but now they raced to save the lives of others.

It happened about October first during a very rainy season. The equinoctial storms had begun about September nineteenth and it had rained almost continually up to the first of October. People on the Crooked Creek ranch had never seen the creek so high before.

This would not have mattered especially to them had it not been for the fact that the spring before a small irrigation company, comprising a dozen farmers eight miles down the creek on the flat open country, had built a dam on Crooked Creek just below the holdings of the ranch. While it was some four miles from the ranch fences, yet it was just outside the unfenced land that the ranch people grazed in the winter time. Even when the water was of normal height this artificial lake set back for a quarter of a mile upon one of the ranch's best meadows, but at the time of high water it flooded nearly half a mile.

The head cow-puncher had sent Larry and Patches down to reconnoiter and to see if conditions were as bad as had been reported to him. Larry had made his way along the southeastern bank of the creek and had climbed the bluffs on that side nearest the dam. He was standing on the very crest of the hilltop looking at the beautiful artificial lake which stretched away up the valley for nearly a mile. This lake was also half a mile wide in some places and quite deep, so it will be seen that the flimsily constructed concrete and boulder dam held back a considerable body of water.

The dam had been hastily constructed by the farmers without very much engineering skill. They had not even copied the cunning of the beaver who curves his dam upstream in the middle in order to distribute the pressure of the water along the entire dam. Instead their dam curved down in the middle and Larry wondered as he looked at it how it had ever managed to hold back the great volume of water behind it. The stones from which it had been built were not even quarried, they were simply boulders of every size and shape held together in a flimsy way by concrete which had been dumped in between them.

The sluice-way was wide open but this did not begin to care for the great volume of water for it poured over the dam two feet deep for its entire length. The water was dark and angry and the whole scene was one of grandeur and mighty power held in check by the ingenuity of man.

Larry was just thinking what a devastating flood would be set loose if this flimsy dam ever gave way when a great boulder near the sluice-way toppled from its place and crashed into the creek below. This seemed to precipitate a sort of land slide or rather a stone slide for one boulder after another went crashing after the first and almost in less time than it takes to tell the entire sluice-way itself rushed out and the water came pouring through a gap twenty feet wide and as many high.

"Gracious!" cried the boy under his breath, "I guess they're in for some water down below."

But the words were barely out of his mouth when

more of the dam gave way, first on one side of the stream and then on the other. It went down like a cobhouse, a piece here and a piece there, and the mighty seething waters came rushing through the break like a demon of destruction. Then in a flash the full significance of what he had seen came home to Larry. The back of the dam had been broken and the rest would go in a few seconds. It meant a terrible flood in the valley below. He knew every rod of this country and his imagination pictured the waters piling up in the narrow canyon which stretched away for three miles below, but most of the farmers lived on the prairie land still further down and then he remembered the Ganzers, the family of floaters who had so annoyed the Crooked Creek ranch people the year before, and who had finally set fire to the lower plateau. This family of squatters had built a cabin two miles below the dam that very spring and so far as he knew they were still there. They were in the immediate pathway of the flood in one of the narrowest portions of the canyon where the water would pile up like a veritable deluge.

It was true that the Ganzers were enemies of the ranch people, but even so he would have to warn them. And was not little Elsie Ganzer one of the family? Elsie and he had been the best of friends all through the feud between her folks and the ranch people the year before. She was only eight years old and the sins of her parents ought not to be visited on her. Larry remembered her just as he had seen her that first summer morning in July when her flaxen hair was streaming in the morning breeze. Her eyes were of heavenly blue and sparkling with pleasure and her cheeks like roses while her mouth was stained red with wild strawberries.

He had taken her upon the pommel of his saddle and given her a ride on Patches' back and they had been good chums from that hour. He could not forsake her now. Patches who was hitched in a clump of aspens a score of rods away was greatly astonished a minute later when his master came tearing through the bushes and sprang into the saddle pulling the reins free from a sapling as he sprang.

Patches could not imagine why his master was in such a hurry. There were no cattle in sight and there was no race on, but he, like the good horse he was, took his cue from his impatient master and they flew down the little bridle path leading to the wagon trail at a breakneck gallop. Larry leaned low over the horse's neck in order to escape a lashing from the limbs of over-hanging trees. The pathway was rough but Paches was used to rough riding and hummocks and depressions did not break their head-long gallop.

In the shortest possible time they had covered the mile to the wagon trail. Larry pulled sharply on the left rein and headed his faithful horse straight up the valley into the teeth of the on-coming flood.

He had not covered half a mile when he met the Ganzer family. They were in their lumber wagon drawn by two frantically galloping horses, but all were not there for as he pulled up beside the wagon, old man Ganzer shouted to him, "Elsie, mine little girl, Elsie, we cannot find her."

"Where is she gone?" inquired Larry incredulously.

"We do not know," wailed Mrs. Ganzer, "we cannot find her."

"Cowards," called Larry back over his shoulder as he gave Patches the quirt and galloped on towards the Ganzer cottage. It did not matter that a torrent of water thirty or forty feet high was rushing down the valley towards them, he must save little Elsie at any cost.

Would he reach the cabin ahead of the flood? Would he have time to look for her if he did? And if he discovered her would they both have time to escape on Patches' back? Such were the thoughts that surged through his brain as he galloped madly up the canyon. In two minutes time he rounded a curve in the draw which gave him an unobstructed view for three hundred yards. Fifty yards ahead was the Ganzer cabin, two-hundred yards beyond that was the avalanche of on-coming waters. It was carrying upon its crest trees,

bushes and all sorts of débris and Larry was aghast at
the height and breadth of the flood. As he neared the
cabin he shouted at the top of his lungs, "Elsie, Elsie,
where are you?" Presently he thought he heard a faint
cry from the bluff at the left and looking in that direction he saw her running hurriedly down the path which
wound out and in among the trees. Her hair was
streaming in the autumn wind and she was pale with
fear, but she still clutched in her hands a bunch of
autumn leaves.

"Run to me, Elsie," Larry called, barely making
himself heard above the roar of the flood which was
now like the sound of continuous thunder. He turned
Patches about so as to be in readiness, but did not dare
dismount and all the time he looked over his shoulder
to watch the on-coming monster. The seconds seemed
like hours, but finally, breathless and excited, Elsie
threw herself against Patches' side and at the same instant Larry caught her by the collar of her coat and set
her upon the saddle in front of him.

"Cling on tight," he warned.

At that instant the advance wave of the flood struck
them. It was foaming, hissing and gnashing its teeth.
The wave was only three or four feet high but it gave
them a good drenching.

Then Larry let the quirt fall on Patches' side and he

"CLING ON TIGHT" HE WARNED

bounded away. "Thank God," the young man thought, "we are safe."

But he had counted his chickens too soon for at that instant he noted that the water on the left side of the draw was racing much faster than that on the right because of fewer obstructions and the crest was much higher on that side. A great wave eight feet high was rushing across the canyon directly towards them, in fact it almost cut off their retreat. Could he get through it in time?

Then the hissing, foaming wave went over their heads and for a moment Larry thought they were lost. He felt Patches lose his footing and flounder in the flood, but that was only for a second for almost immediately he regained his foothold and burst out of the waters that sought to engulf them, like an express train and was racing down the valley at his best pace. With each hundred feet that he covered he left the water thirty feet behind. When Larry had seen the flood recede to one hundred feet he felt a little safer, but even so the race was a desperate one. If Patches were to slip on a rolling stone or stumble, even the slipping of the saddle or the breaking of a cinch might be fatal. But none of these things happened and rod by rod the fine horse drew away from the on-coming flood and by the time they reached the prairie land at the mouth of the draw the flood had been left far behind. Here they overtook the Ganzers in their lumber wagon.

"Here she is," cried Larry as he reined Patches up beside the wagon. "She is wet as a drowned rat but safe and sound."

"Gott in heaven bless you," cried Mrs. Ganzer,

weeping and laughing, as she hugged the child to her breast, "my baby, my baby."

"Gott bless you, my boy," said old man Ganzer in his broken English. "I am ashamed that I have been so mean to you cattle people."

"You don't any of you deserve such a sweet little girl after deserting her in that cowardly way," said Larry, "but take good care of her now you have her back."

Then he galloped away and they heard his clear, resonant voice like a bugle call as it echoed far over the prairie land.

"The dam has burst. The flood is upon you. Look to your lives and your live stock."

Thanks to Larry's timely warning the people of the little settlement on the prairie saved their own lives as well as those of their horses and cattle although they lost a few chicken coops and pig pens and some small stock. But the story of the young man's daring rescue of Elsie Ganzer in the face of the on-coming flood and his heroic warning of the people in the settlement spread like wild fire through the region. If anything more was needed to add to the fame of this wonderful horse and his intrepid rider this story did it.

CHAPTER XIV

GOOD NIGHT WYOMING

THREE friends of the once famous cow-puncher polo team sat in the smoker of the Rocky Mountain Limited as the long train coasted down the shiny rails close to the foot-hills of the Sierra Madre mountains on the way to Wyanne. These friends were Pony Perkins, Long Tom and Larry. Pony and Tom were playing pitch while Larry sat in the seat next to them looking rather wistfully out of the window. They were passing through the sage brush country, the land of the purple sage or whispering sage if you happened to be in poetic mood. He was thinking how much more beautiful was the Crooked Creek country back in the mountains than was this land of sage brush.

Presently Pony paused in shuffling the cards and said, "I hev been thinkin' ever since we boarded this here flyer that there's one gent missing in this here party. Our company ain't complete. Of course, I am thinkin' of Big Bill."

"Pony, you get out," ejaculated Long Tom, "jest as if we didn't know of whom you was thinkin'. Why, I hev been thinkin' of him ever since we been here play-

259

ing cards. That's the reason I played my jack on your ace the last hand in that fool way cause I was thinkin' of Bill."

"I have been thinking of him all day," said Larry wistfully. "Hardly a day passes but what I think of him in some way."

"Well you may," said Pony, "for he looked upon you almost as a son and he was as proud as Lucifer of your way with a hoss."

"What a whale he would have been with a mechette! What a swath he would have mowed among the dons if he'd got into this here enterprise!" put in Long Tom.

"I am thinkin' there won't be much mechette business in this," returned Pony. "I guess it will be all long range rifles. I don't even think our .45's will be of much use unless it comes to a close-up brush with the dons."

At this point in the conversation Pony and Long Tom resumed their game and Larry returned to his looking out of the window. He well remembered the first night he had seen this sage brush country. He had thought it the most monotonous sight in the world with its endless grays and dull browns. But to-night as he saw it in the gathering shadows of the late afternoon he rather liked it although it could not compare with the mesas and canyons up in the Crooked Creek country.

As he sat there by the window he recalled how this strange adventure had all come about. It seemed to him more like a weird dream than a stern reality in his own young life.

Two weeks before he had been sent down to Wyanne on business by his uncle. He had been sitting in a restaurant one morning eating bacon and eggs and drinking hot coffee when as he happened to pick up a newspaper while he was waiting for more bacon, his eye fell upon an account of the hideous atrocity in Cuba. Some Spanish soldiers had captured half a dozen unfortunate peons and in order to get these Cubans to reveal the whereabouts of General Garcia's army they had crushed their hands and feet in a cane-crushing mill on a sugar plantation. As Larry pictured this hideous scene his eyes filled with tears and to cover his embarrassment he arose and went to the window. The first thing that his eyes fell upon as he looked across the street was Old Glory waving above the recruiting office just over the way. The beautiful flag was rising and falling in the morning wind and as Larry beheld it he thought it the most beautiful thing he had ever seen in the whole world; and when he remembered that this flag sheltered one hundred million happy people and that it protected every citizen in the land, rich or poor, his love for the flag which he had always worshipped redoubled; and without stopping to think what he was doing he walked out of the restaurant, crossed the street to the recruiting office and wrote down his name as one of Colonel Roosevelt's Rough Riders.

When the deed had been done he went back to the restaurant and finished his coffee and paid his bill. When he had told his uncle of the step on returning to the ranch, at first Hank Brodie had looked very serious, then he had embraced his nephew and kissed him as tenderly on the cheek as his own mother could have done.

"Son," he said, "I always knew you had good stuff in you, but of course I did not dream it would come to this."

Then Larry sought out his two friends, Pony and Long Tom, and told them. They had both clapped him on the shoulder and told him it was all right. A few minutes later, after consulting Hank Brodie, they had mounted their horses and ridden away. When Larry asked his uncle where they had gone he smiled and said, "Oh, they've gone down to Wyanne to enlist."

So here they were, the three Crooked Creek cow-punchers on their way to Wyanne where they were to join half a dozen other brave fellows and the little party was to make its way to San Antonio and thence to Cuba.

"Who is this here Theodore Roosevelt that is going

to be our Lieutenant Colonel?" inquired Long Tom
as he gathered up the cards and began shuffling.

"Why, don't you know," returned Pony who was
something of a reader, "why, he's a rich New York
gent and if all we read about him is true he's a real
guy. Why, he scared the entire New York police force
out of their boots when he was police commissioner.
Then he came out to northwestern Missouri and went
into the ranch business. He's a regular cow-puncher,
he is, and the bad men of Missouri were as afraid of
him as good folks are of the devil. He's a regular guy
all right and we can bank on him."

"He's good enough for me, then," replied Long
Tom.

"Me, too," said Larry.

Presently as Larry noted that his friends had begun
another rubber he arose and said casually, "If you
gents will excuse me for a few minutes guess I will
go back to the observation car. I want to see the sun
sink behind the old Sierras once more and I want to
say good-night to the Wyoming hills."

"That's right, son," said Long Tom, "allus stick to
your colors and be faithful to the homeland."

"So long, Larry," said Pony affectionately, "we'll
meet you in half an hour in the dining car."

To his great joy Larry found the observation car
entirely deserted and he sat down where he had a

splendid view of the Sierras away to the southwest.
The sun still stood about fifteen minutes above the
horizon's rim and the full blaze of its departing glory
fell upon the foothills some eight or ten thousand feet
below the mountains' crest. This radiant splendor of
the sunlight shed such a glory over the foothills that
they looked like ancient battlements with little minarets
and domes of gold. But soon the light receded up the
mountain side and dark shadows took its place over
the hills. Larry could plainly discern the dark blue-
green of the forest and he knew his old friends, the
pines, the spruces, the cedars, and the hemlocks, were
there in all their dark mystic beauty. But once more
the advancing shadows forced the sunlight to retreat
to the mountains' crest and the full glory of departing
day was seen along the top of the range upon the snow
and ice fields that still lingered on the caps of the
highest peaks. Then the mountain top for twenty miles
became a gorgeous rainbow, so bright that the eye could
scarce behold it. But the shadows still pursued and
almost before the full beauty had been realized the
lower side of the rainbow had faded and shadows took
its place. Up, up the legions of darkness pursued until
a dark red band on the horizon's rim had succeeded the
rainbow. But still the shadows pursued and soon the
dark red faded into crimson, the crimson into pink, the
pink into lighter pink, until finally all color had faded

out and an aurora of white light streamed upward into the sky from the point where the sun had disappeared.

Larry had been deeply moved by the wonder of the spectacle and as the last vestige of color faded, a little cry escaped him. "My God, how I love it all," he said under his breath. "These mountains, and the hills, and the canyons and the rivers. There is nothing I know of like it in the whole world."

Then he covered his eyes with his hands and said reverently, "God bless Wyoming and guard these hills and Crooked Creek ranch until I come again."

The ranch was now hidden from sight some forty or fifty miles behind the mountains, but Larry could still see in memory the long gray ranch buildings with the friendly old cottonwoods keeping guard above them. How well he knew every season upon the ranch; the spring time with the hundreds of little white-faced calves playing on the green carpet of the mesa and vying with the homely little colts in their capers; the summer time with its wild strawberries, wild plums and service berries, and with its wild roses. He had never seen such wild roses anywhere else in the whole world. They clambered over fallen logs and boulders and even up the sides of the canyons. And then in the autumn time there was the goldenrod and asters. Where else in the world was such vital vibrant color as during this season when Piñon birds and magpies flocked for their southern flight. Then winter with its endless snow and biting wind, and the stern music of howling coyotes and howling winds had a peculiar beauty all its own. And this beautiful country which for four years he had called home was fading, fading, fading; it was slipping away from him at the rate of fifty miles an hour. When would he see it again?

Now although the last shimmer of light which showed where the sun had sunk a few minutes before had disappeared and night had let down her dusky mantle, yet Larry knew that far away in Piñon Valley the sun was still shining.

And Patches, faithful Patches who would have run until he dropped for his master, knew even better than Larry did that the sun was shining in Piñon Valley, for he was standing at the lower end of the valley in the full blaze of departing day with his head up, his ears thrust forward, his eyes bright, and his nostrils extended. He seemed to be waiting, or looking, or listening for something. It was a picture that would have delighted the eye of a Remington or a Rosa Bonheur. Who shall say that Patches did not receive a message, or that he did not feel the great wave of love and admiration that welled up in his master's heart for him as he turned to leave the observation car and rejoin his friends at dinner? It is not for us humans to say this was not so, for we are continually making new discov-

eries in the world of animal psychology which amaze
us. Presently the spell was broken and without warning Patches wheeled like a flash and raced up the valley at a wild gallop and a minute later disappeared
through the cul-de-sac on his way to the upper mesa.

The upper mesa had been the favorite feeding ground
of the wild horses for a long time before man ever
came to Wyoming with his countless cattle. The grass
was sweeter there than anywhere else on the ranch and
Patches knew this fact full well. The water in Crooked
Creek up there was clear and cool, and in the summer
time when it was hot on the mesa the shade in Aspen
Draw was cool and refreshing. So Patches was going
back to the wild and once again he would be a free
horse ranging in the hills just as his wild kindred had
done in years gone by. Once again he would come
and go at will with no hand to bridle or saddle him for
Larry had given orders that he should not be ridden
or driven until he returned. So his life was once more
his own just as it had been before he had been broken
and he was as free to come and go as the wandering
wind.

And who should say when that master would return?
He had gone upon stern business. But even Larry's
most enthusiastic admirers and ardent well-wishers
could not have guessed that he would be back within
sixty days without a scratch from bullet or shrapnel.

If his eyes were sunken and his cheeks hollow and he had lost twenty pounds during the campaign, what did that matter, he was still strong and vigorous and as ready for the storms of life as a young oak for the blasts of winter. Not only this but he had brought back with him the added distinction of being Lieutenant Larry Winton and a close friend of the impetuous Colonel.

THE END